JACK'S HANDY GUIDE TO BASEBALL JARGON

Go Yard! With Baseball Slang

By
Jack Forbes

JAFO PUBLISHING
2010 West Avenue K, PMB 520
Lancaster, CA 93536

JACK'S HANDY GUIDE TO BASEBALL JARGON
Go Yard! With Baseball Slang

Copyright © 2025

ISBN: 978-0-9997069-3-0 (Paperback Edition)
ISBN: 978-09997069-2-3 (Ebook/Kindle Edition)

Published in the United States by
JAFO PUBLISHING

Printed in the United States of America

Contact website information:
www.JafoPublishing.com

DISCLAIMER: This book is a work of fiction as applied to baseball
rules and jargon. Although the author attempts to portray the jargon
and rules of baseball with substantial accuracy, the names, characters,
baseball teams and incidents portrayed herein are the work of the
author's imagination. Any resemblance to actual persons, living or
dead, baseball teams, events or localities is entirely coincidental.

TABLE OF CONTENTS

PREFACE

My first contact with baseball was playing catch with my father in Long Beach, California. As I recall, I was about four years old at the time. The ball was a 9-inch softball, which resembled a real baseball but was softer and lighter and wouldn't hurt as badly if I missed a catch. It *would* break a window, however, which I found out the hard way, one afternoon.

My dad and I played catch literally every day, and if it were up to me, we would never stop until it was too dark outside to see. Inevitably, however, my mother called us in for dinner and we would continue to throw a few more before walking inside for a delicious meal. My mother was an amazing cook!

When I was six years old, I joined a team in a "Tee-shirt" league of baseball. We were the *Belmont Bombers* and our home field was the local Junior High School known as Rogers Junior High in Long Beach, California. *Go Mustangs!* The league played with a nine-inch softball. My father had previously hit grounders and pop-ups to me by that time, and I was tried out in a few different positions on the team. The outfield didn't work so well, however, since my break (now called a "jump") for the fly-ball was late each time. I didn't know it then, but I badly needed eyeglasses for distance vision. By the time I saw the flight of the ball, it was well on its way, making it tough to get to where I needed to be in order to catch it. In fact, believe it or not, I didn't find out I needed glasses until my eyesight was tested for my learner's permit driver's license when I was 15 ½ years old! I'll never forget walking outside wearing a pair of horn-rimmed glasses (I hated the look) and seeing *individual leaves* on trees for the first time from a distance. I said to my mother, "*That's what people can see?!*"

Anyway, back to my Belmont Bombers experience. So, they tried me out in the infield and finally I could see the ball clearly.

I moved on grounders and pop-ups very well. From that day on, I was an infielder, shortstop to be precise, for the Belmont Bombers. I loved baseball.

My dad also taught me how to hit the ball and would pitch buckets to me at a local dirt diamond. He had been a Varsity tennis player in college and never played baseball, but he had an accurate throw and could send strikes repeatedly. After batting 30 or so balls, I'd run around the field, putting 'em back into the bucket for another round. His classic advice to me in batting was: "Keep your eye on the ball, Jackie." He had the best of intentions and was instrumental in the beginning of my baseball career in helping me to understand how to hit a pitched ball.

My family would regularly go over to Chavez Ravine and watch the Dodgers play. The Dodgers had just moved to Los Angeles from Brooklyn and I got to see some of the greats of the day play there, including Pee Wee Reese, Duke Snyder, Don Drysdale and Sandy Koufax. When the Cardinals came to town, I watched Stan "the Man" Musial play. He was an icon to me and since those days, I've always had been a fan of the Cardinals, unless, of course, they're playing the Dodgers!

After youth baseball, I laid off several years before discovering that there was something known as Sunday Baseball (Long Beach, California) and the Men's Adult Baseball League (Orange County, California). I started playing in those leagues in 1983 and continued for a total of 13 seasons. I always played in the unlimited division, where there was no minimum age for the adult players. These were not "Senior" leagues by any means. In each team on which I played (except on *The Naturals, see* below), all of the players were in their 20s, except for me, in my 30s to 40s. Players in the leagues were mostly retired college ballplayers, and retired Major and Minor League players. Most of the time, I played Second Base or Third Base, but towards the end of my amateur baseball career, I played the Center Field and First Base positions. At the batting cages, on many, many occasions, I used Charlie Lau's book, *The Art of Hitting .300*, with illustrative photos of George Brett, to train myself to be an exceptionally effective hitter.

In 1984, I started a team called *The Naturals*. The founding members were myself, Jerry Scanlan, Jeff Severson and Joe Jennings. Joe had just graduated from USC and had been a starting pitcher there. Jeff had just finished a stalwart career as a Defensive Safety in the National Football League, and Jerry Scanlan was a future international-caliber softball player in various Senior Softball travel teams. We recruited players from all of our respective contacts and had a roster to knock your socks off. The team practiced twice a week, every week, before our Sunday games. I played Second Base the entire season. Jeff was excellent at Shortstop. Jerry ("Scan Man") was a great catch and virtual cannon in Right Field, and Joe was our star Hurler. We had another fireball pitcher nicknamed "Bama" from Alabama, and a Black Belt karate fighter, Bob Mitchell camping out at First Base. Our catcher, whose name escapes me, had a rocket arm for throwing out the occasional, hapless, baserunner trying to steal Second. Our entire roster was talented and we had a fabulously successful season. We had a mailed weekly newsletter touching on our past game, updating our player stats and previewing the upcoming game, game-time and field.

Occasionally we got to play at Blair Field, which was the equivalent of playing at a Single-A Minor League ballpark (seating capacity: around 5,000). In fact, Blair Field is where many of the baseball scenes from the film, *Money Ball*, were later filmed.

The Naturals won *every single game* of the entire regular season, and lost only in the final Championship game between the American and National Leagues. (Controversial, bad call by the Blue, but, of course, that's long been water under the bridge [not really forgotten at all, as you can see!].)

Those thirteen seasons were great days, complete with glorious wins and some disappointing defeats. I had my share of minor setbacks with injuries of one sort or another, but for the most part and thankfully, I emerged from this phase of my athletic career completely healthy.

Over the years, I noticed that the language used in, and in describing, baseball was heavily loaded with slang terms *vital for knowing the game itself.* Unfortunately, without a life-long background in baseball, it's difficult to understand the many complicated situations which routinely arise in the course of baseball.

I'm aware that there are already a few books on the subject of baseball jargon (including tedious description of origins of terms or somewhat dry examples of use). There are also several online glossaries of terms (some short, some longer, some organized alphabetically, some by baseball subject matter). But there were no books with a *comprehensive, though selective*, list of baseball terms, *clear descriptions* of meanings, and *entertaining examples* of use. Until now.

So, I decided to add this collection, of baseball jargon and usage, to my litany of books on the enormously rich English Language. To all of my wonderful Readers I say, "*Play Ball!*" and please enjoy this heartfelt tribute to my favorite American pastime, Baseball.

Jack Forbes
Author

#

A 1-2-3 Inning

Meaning: Any inning where the Pitcher retires three Batters in a row without any of the Batters safely reaching base.

> *With the bang-bang play at first base, and much to the relief of Manager Stan Snell, the Daisy Dukes finally had a 1-2-3 inning.*

1 (through) 9

Meaning: On defense, for ease of scoring, each player is assigned a number, as follows: Pitcher-1; Catcher-2; First-baseman-3; Second-baseman-4; Third-baseman-5; Shortstop-6; Left-fielder-7; Center-fielder-8; and, Right-fielder-9.

> *One-hopper to Swenson at Short and a 6-4-3 double play for outs one and two in the first.*

A

Aboard

Meaning: Any Batter who successfully reaches any base.

Reginal Smith's face lit up when he ran out the nubber and found himself aboard on first.

Ace

Meaning: A particularly effective Pitcher.

Smokin' Joe Jennings was indisputably the Ace for the Long Beach Naturals.

Advance the Runner

Meaning: A batting strategy, such as laying down a bunt, to move a baserunner successfully to the next base.

With no outs, Clyde McNally's mission was to advance the runner to third base, and he accomplished just that.

Ahead/Behind/Even on the Count

Meaning: A Batter is ahead on the count if at any given time there are more balls than strikes but, in that event, the Pitcher is behind on the count, and *vice versa*, while if there are the same number of balls and strikes, both the Batter and the Pitcher are even on the count.

Ahead on the count, Bryce Matthews was sitting on a four-seam fastball, and he got his wish, and then some.

Airmail

Meaning: When a fielder makes a throw that flies high above and out of reach of the intended recipient Player.

> *Shortstop Percy Peterson airmailed his throw to first base, allowing the runner on second to advance to third base.*

An at 'Em Ball

Meaning: A ball that is batted almost directly at a fielder.

> *It was an at 'em ball to Short from the word "go," and the runner was out by a country mile.*

Around the Horn

Meaning: With less than three outs and no one on base, and if an out is made (for example, a Batter strikes out), this describes when the Catcher throws the ball to one of various infielders as a celebration and to keep their arms warmed up. The usual sequence of throws is from the Catcher to the Third-baseman, to the Shortstop, to the Second-baseman, to the Third-baseman, who then tosses it to the Pitcher.

> *The Minnesota Miners celebrated their thrilling double play by briskly tossing the game ball around the horn.*

At-bat(s)

Meaning: For statistical purposes, an at-bat is considered to have occurred when a hitter strikes out, reaches base from a hit, an error (other than Catcher's interference), or a fielder's choice, or when he is thrown or put out on a non-sacrifice.

Despite the fielder's choice, Reginal Jones took his at-bat in stride, settling into his customary 15-foot lead, off first.

At the Corners

Meaning: Regarding *pitched balls*: at any of the four corners of the imaginary, rectangular strike zone.

Carlson swiftly retired the cleanup hitter by meticulously pitching two sliders and a screwball at the corners.

At the Corners/Runners at First and Third

Meaning: Regarding *runners on base*: baserunners simultaneously and only on both first base and third base.

With runners at the corners and a tie-ball game, the Southpaw calmly went into his stretch, seemingly oblivious to the threat looming just off third base.

At the Letters

Meaning: A pitched ball crossing the plate above the strike zone, in the vicinity of the team's name on the Player's jersey.

Nicholson habitually fell behind on the count through his tendency to swing at fastballs at the letters.

Away/Outside

Meaning: When a pitch is outside the strike zone, to the far side of the plate with respect to the Batter.

Plate Umpire softly murmured "Ball" when the slider missed away.

Away Game/Road Game

Meaning: A game or games which take(s) place at the opponent's home field.

The Vermont Vipers headed out of town on a less-than-luxury bus for a series of away games with their arch rivals, the New England Nordics.

Away Team/Visiting Team/Road Team

Meaning: The team which plays at the opponent's home field, bats in the top of the innings and wears gray, as opposed to white, uniforms.

The Rattlers were happy to be the road team in their battle with the Dirt Devils, considering the fair weather in Long Beach, California.

B

Backdoor Slider

Meaning: A pitch that heads out of the strike zone but then turns back, over an edge of the plate.

With the count 2-2, the lefty, Eddie Wexler, was looking for anything to hit, but froze on a backdoor slider for strike three.

Backwards K

Meaning: A strike out looking.

Ace Billy Billington racked up four Ks and three backwards Ks in his outing today.

Bad Call

Meaning: An Umpire's call which is clearly incorrect or unfair as to the Umpire's judgment, proper interpretation of rules or position to see a given play. *See,* Make-up Call

The Ump's bad call sent the Newfoundland Ganders into a tail spin, no pun intended, in their lopsided loss to the Gloucester Guppies, 15-zip.

Bad Hop

Meaning: Where a thrown or batted ball takes an unexpected bounce, making it much more difficult to catch by the defensive Player.

Sorenson had a great jump on the ball, but the bad hop sent it careening into left field for a base hit.

Bag(s)/Base(s)

Meaning: The physical, square, tightly packed objects secured at the corners of a baseball diamond, which represent the four stations to which Players can run or advance, or score runs—namely: first base, second base, third base and the hard-rubber, pentagonal-shaped home (normally referred to as home plate or simply, the plate). (See also, Dish).

> *Elmo Perkins was called "out," on appeal, for failing to touch the bag at second in his grandiose home run trot.*

Balk

Meaning: With one or more runners on base, an action by a Pitcher which is not allowed under the rules due to its tendency to unfairly deceive or manipulate runners, resulting, when called, in all runners advancing one base.

> *The crowd erupted in celebration when Jim Johnson committed a walk-off balk, advancing the runner at third to home in the bottom of the ninth.*

Ball/Baseball

Meaning: The official form of the spherical object used as a ball in the game of baseball.

> *My father's classic batting advice to me as a boy was to keep my, "eye on the ball."*

Ball/Called Ball

Meaning: a pitched baseball which is called a "ball" by the Umpire, as neither striking the Batter's bat nor passing through the strike zone over the plate.

Percy Smithers drew his second walk, as the scroogie missed and ball four was called.

Ballpark/Stadium

Meaning: The overall structure and playing field where the game of baseball is played.

Mary-Ellen and her beau, Tommy, jumped into their '52 Chevy and headed out for a day at the ballpark.

Baltimore Chop

Meaning: A ground ball that is hit so sharply down that it often bounces over an infielder's head.

Winston Pennypacker had come up empty in the three previous at-bats, but with this Baltimore Chop, he reached first safely.

Bang-bang Play

Meaning: A force-play at one of the bases where the ball arrives to the fielder almost simultaneously with the runner touching the bag.

Sure to be appealed regardless of the call, it was a bang-bang play and according to the Umpire, the runner was...safe!

Baseball Glove/Mitt

Meaning: A padded, leather covering for the non-throwing hand to facilitate catching (or concealing) a batted or thrown ball.

6-year-old Ronnie Sparks was thrilled to find a brand new, infielder's baseball glove under the tree on Christmas morning, from his Dad and Mom.

Baseball Man/Scout

Meaning: A man who grew up playing baseball, played some professional baseball as an adult, whose life is inexorably intertwined with the game of baseball and the performance of baseball Players, and who works at discovering and signing talented prospects for a particular professional baseball team.

Washington was a baseball man, not some outsider trained in statistics and union rules, and when he signed high school senior Pete Honeycutt, it made all the traveling and long days worthwhile.

Base Hit/Single

Meaning: A Batter's hit into fair territory that is not caught on the fly, from which he reaches base safely, other than as a result of a fielding error or a fielder's choice.

Porter really CRUSHED that ball, arriving safely at first with a base hit.

Base on Balls/Free Pass/Walk

Meaning: When a Batter is pitched four, called balls, or designated by the opposing team as a walk.

> *Preferring to take their chances with Swifty Baker, the on-deck Batter, they pitched Big Jim Thomas four balls just outside the strike zone, for the walk.*

Base Paths

Meaning: These are the lanes within which baserunners must stay when moving between the bases; three-feet in width between home and first and between third and home, although to and from second base, there is no set width.

> *During the rundown, and prior to any tag, the Ump called the Coyotes' baserunner out for traveling outside of the base path.*

Baserunner/Runner

Meaning: A Player on offense who is on, leading off from, or moving toward any base.

> *The Sidewinders' baserunner made a full-speed, head-first slide toward home, but was tagged out by the skillful Catcher.*

Bases Loaded/Loaded

Meaning: Baserunners on first, second and third base and two or fewer outs.

With the bases loaded, and down three runs in the bottom of the ninth, the young slugger from Louisville, Kentucky stepped into the Batter's box, ready to go yard.

Basket Catch

Meaning: A type of discouraged and often unreliable underhand catch where the glove is extended, pocket facing upwards, catching a fly ball as if in a basket.

Mulrooney tempted fate every time he made a basket catch in the outfield, and until today, he'd never dropped a single attempt.

Bat/Baseball Bat/Wood (noun)

Meaning: A smooth wooden (or metal, outside of professional baseball) club, of particular authorized dimensions, used in baseball to hit a pitched ball.

To Manuel Sanchez, his well-balanced, 33-inch, drop-3, handcrafted maple bat felt like a musical instrument in his capable hands, and Pitchers well knew of his prowess at the plate.

Bat (verb)

Meaning: During an at-bat, for the hitter to attempt to safely reach one or more bases and/or to advance a baserunner, without being thrown out or tagged out, and doing so by a hit-by-pitch, a walk, or hitting a pitched ball into fair territory without the ball being caught on the fly.

Frosty was up to bat and represented the tying run in a four-three ballgame.

Bat Around

Meaning: In any given half-inning, if each Player in the lineup, of the team on offense, has completed a plate appearance and the first Batter of that half-inning comes up to bat for a second time.

The San Berdu Smoke Jumpers batted around in the fifth, stranded three and scored four runs.

Bat Boy/Bat Girl

Meaning: A person, wearing a team uniform, employed by a baseball team to retrieve a Batter's bat and other equipment after an at-bat, or to field out-of-play ground balls in foul territory.

The bat girl knocked down an ugly finder that had ricocheted around the Hound Dogs dugout.

Bat Flip/Flipped (one's) Bat

Meaning: A Batter flipping his bat up and over after going yard.

Before his home run even left the yard, Kingsley flipped his bat.

Bat Shaving/Shaved Bat

Meaning: An illegal practice of shaving the inside of a bat (primarily, of a composite bat) in order to attempt to improve its performance by enhancing the rebound factor.

Upon contact with the 4-seam fastball, Parker's shaved bat exploded, sending a shower of composite shards toward the bump.

Batter/Hitter

Meaning: The Player at the plate attempting to advance to first base or further without making an out or to advance another runner.

The Batter kicked dirt from between his cleats, adjusted his glasses and helmet and stepped into the Batter's box with bad intentions.

Batter's Box/Box

Meaning: The chalk-lined, rectangular marking to either side of the plate, entirely within which a Batter must stand when receiving a pitch.

Benny Black called time and stepped out of the Batter's box to wipe sweat from his eyes.

Batter Up!

Meaning: A rarely utilized Plate Umpire's direction for a Batter to step into the Batter's box at the beginning of the game or of an inning.

In the old days of baseball, Plate Umpires commonly cried out, "Batter up!", but in today's pro ball, this is rarely if ever heard.

The **Battery**

Meaning: Rather than being considered as infielders, the Pitcher and Catcher of a team comprise what is known as the Battery.

Tonight, the Eagles' Battery consists of Roberts on the hill and Mendoza behind the dish.

Batting Average

Meaning: The percentage, expressed as a three-digit decimal, of a hitter's at-bats which result in base hits or extra base hits.

Hawk had a respectable batting average of .285, but his slugging percentage was over .600!

Batting Gloves

Meaning: Leather gloves, sometimes padded on the back of the hands, worn by most Batters in order to provide grip and prevent blisters or impact injuries.

Houser's padded batting glove saved him from a broken left hand by the high and tight pitch.

Batting Order

Meaning: The sequence of Batters which is written into the lineup, and as amended by substitutions during the game.

The batting order had been set since the night before, and Willie "Longball" Jones was batting cleanup.

Beanball

Meaning: A pitch deliberately thrown by a Pitcher towards the head of a Batter.

> *Dolan was a notorious beanball Pitcher, but tonight the Sparrows finally said, "Enough is enough."*

Benches Clear

Meaning: when the Players from both teams suddenly burst onto the field of play, typically responding to a perceived gross violation of the unwritten rules of baseball etiquette.

> *After Simmon's knockdown pitch, Kraeger charged the mound and both benches cleared.*

Bleachers

Meaning: The raised, tiered rows of benches, sometimes with back support, directly beyond the left and right fields.

> *This one's a no doubter deep into the left-field bleachers, and just like that, the Sidewinders are up, one nothing in the top of the first inning.*

Bleeder

Meaning: A ground ball hit so weekly that it commonly results in an infield base hit.

> *Baker hits a bleeder down the third baseline, but with the troubles he's had recently, he's happy to be aboard.*

Bloop Single/Dying Quail/Texas Leaguer/Blooper

Meaning: A pop-up hit just beyond the reach of infielders and too shallow for any outfielder to catch the ball on the fly.

A vicious swing but under the ball and that will be...a Texas Leaguer base hit for Mooney.

Blow a Save/Blown Save

Meaning: For a Relief Pitcher, in a save situation, to allow an opposing team to score the tying run or more, even as a result of fielding errors.

And all it took for Zander's third blown save of the season is one, untimely wild pitch, as the tying run scored from third base.

Boot (the ball)/Kick

Meaning: When a fielder, in the process of fielding a ground ball, inadvertently kicks the ball away.

What would have been a single, turns into a stand-up double as Center-fielder Juan Garcia boots away a grounder.

Box Score

Meaning: A chart used in baseball, presenting statistical data about Player performance in a particular game.

The box score gave raw data about the Tiger's win, but it failed to reveal the virtual thrill-ride afforded its fans.

Breaking Up a Double Play/Take-out Slide

Meaning: When an advancing runner slides or otherwise maneuvers in the base path so as to, in some manner, legally defeat an attempted double play.

> *Peterson attempted to break up the double play with a cleats-high slide into second base, and immediately, a rhubarb erupted between him and Shortstop, Bobby Brooks.*

Bronx Cheer

Meaning: When the crowd is booing or otherwise ridiculing a Player.

> *The Bakersfield fans greeted the Lancaster Catcher with the Bronx Cheer whenever he batted.*

Brushback Pitch (*see also*, Up and In)

Meaning: A high and tight fastball, intended by the Pitcher to deter the Batter from crowding the plate.

> *Garret Moore threw a fastball inside and at the letters as a brushback pitch, to set up the next low and outside slider.*

Building a Fence

Meaning: When a baseball team scores in multiple one-run innings, the scoreboard begins to resemble a picket fence, like 1 1 1 1 1 1

> *The scrappy Mojave Prairie Dogs built a fence on the scoreboard with their short-ball tactics.*

Bullpen/Pen

Meaning: The area of a ballpark designated for a team's Relief Pitchers to warm up prior to entry into the game.

While Penrose was warming up in the Bears' bullpen, he reached up and caught a home run hit by his own teammate, Shortstop, Sly Masters.

Bunt

Meaning: When the bat is held forward and by the Batter's hands somewhat apart, and the pitched ball is hit as softly as possible in order to make it difficult for infielders to field the ball and make a play.

Batter Vernon Pickering peered over to the Third Base Coach and spotted his team's sign for a bunt—touch of the cap, then touch of the chin.

Bunt Single

Meaning: A bunt resulting to the Batter safely arriving at first, when not a fielder's choice.

Maurice would have settled for the RBI, but to run it out for a bunt single was icing on the cake.

Bush League

Meaning: A derogatory comment in baseball that a particular tactic or action violates unwritten rules of fair and respectful play.

Marcus first heard of his release on waivers on a radio broadcast, and that Buffalo Bobcat's stunt was nothing short of Bush League.

c

Called Game

Meaning: When the Umpire-in-chief determines that a game must be stopped due to conditions which render continuing the game not feasible.

Due to an increasing risk of standing water on the playing field, the game was called for a total of one hour and forty-seven minutes, and then resumed as the storm blew over and the grounds crew uncovered the infield.

Called Strike

Meaning: Considered to be a strike because, although the Batter did not swing, the Umpire called it a strike as crossing the plate within the strike zone.

In his fourth and final at-bat, the called strike on Center-fielder Whitey Moore set him down with an o'fer for the day.

Called Up for a Cup of Coffee

Meaning: When a Player from the Minors is sent up to the associated Major League club for a short stint and then returned to the Minors.

Eddie Yates was thrilled to be called up for a cup of coffee with the Sacramento Bees, and the money wasn't bad neither!

Camping Out

Meaning: Where a fielder, with intel on a Batter, has moved to a particular spot in his defensive position, and is waiting for the Batter to hit to where he is expected to hit.

Hernandez was camping out in left-center field, and his wishes were granted when the long out fell right into his outstretched glove.

Cannon/Gun

Meaning: A particularly strong arm of any Player.

Jerry "ScanMan" Scanlan had a cannon for an arm, and struck fear in the hearts of any runners testing his throw from right field.

Can 'O Corn

Meaning: Any routine fly ball, easily caught with normal skill.

The fly ball to left was a can o' corn for Gold Glove, Josh Farmington.

Cash-in

Meaning: Where a team scores from one or more baserunners on base.

Upton unleashes on that change-up and the Lions cash-in on their runners at second and third!

Catcher/Receiver/Backstop

Meaning: The Player behind home plate who receives pitches from the Pitcher.

The Woodpeckers' backstop is having his work cut out for him today, with no fewer than seven pitches in the dirt and three wild pitches in only four innings of play!

Catcher's Mitt/Catcher's Glove

Meaning: A leather, roundish, strategically padded, fielding glove, without open finger slots, particularly designed for the Catcher in catching or blocking various pitches thrown by a Pitcher and protecting the Catcher's hand.

Despite exceptional padding, hard-thrower Ernest McGill is testing the adequacy of Yeager's Catcher mitt.

Caught Looking

Meaning: When a Batter has two strikes and then fails to swing on a called strike.

And Kadri is caught looking for the final out of the ballgame.

Caught Napping

Meaning: When a baserunner is picked off by the Pitcher or Catcher due to too far of a lead, too slow of a reaction back to the base, or inattention.

A snap throw by Kevin Reynolds and Kerrane is caught napping for the second out of the inning!

Caught Stealing

Meaning: When a baserunner attempts a steal, but is tagged out by the defensive Player taking the throw from (almost always) the Catcher.

Reynoso throws a bullet and just like that, Billings is caught stealing in a close play at second.

Center Field/Center

Meaning: The outfield area in the baseball game field of play, between left field and right field.

Peterson looks up, tries to find the ball, but the sun is glaring down at him in center field and the ball lands fifteen feet away, for a stand-up double.

Center-fielder

Meaning: The position Player for a particular team, assigned to play in center field during a game.

At a full run and in a spectacular, diving, shoestring catch, Center-fielder Steve Landis robs Fred Underhill of a Dying Quail base hit.

Changeup

Meaning: A slower pitch, designed to appear, to the Batter, to be faster.

Robertson is way ahead of the change up, which crossed the plate at a paltry 82 miles an hour.

Charge

Meaning: A fielder reacts to where a ground ball is hit, and moves forward to field it more quickly than if he were to simply wait for the ball to get to him.

With the corners playing up, Third-baseman Elroy Nimitz charges the bunt, throwing a strike to first for the out.

Charged (to a Pitcher)

Meaning: Runs scored which are statistically assigned to a Pitcher under the rules of baseball, regardless of whether scored while he is still on the mound, or scored *after* he has been replaced by another Pitcher, but for which he is nevertheless deemed responsible.

A double to left-center field off York's four-seamer, and the two scoring baserunners will be charged to Benson.

Charge the Mound

Meaning: When a Batter is so incensed by a Pitcher's behavior or by his pitches that he rushes from the Batter's box to the mound with bad intentions.

Westerfeld charged the mound and both benches cleared for the inevitable rhubarb.

Chase (a pitch)

Meaning: Where a Batter swings at a pitched ball that is not in the strike zone, and misses.

Upshaw chases a slider to fill up the count.

Chatter

Meaning: Rapid, sometimes meaningless, and even rhythmic talk by either the offensive or defensive Players, designed to either encourage their own Players or disturb the opposing Players.

By the second inning, the Blue was not amused by the incessant dugout chatter and verbally warned the Manager of the Beaumont Bills to zip it or be ejected.

Check Swing (noun)

Meaning: Where a Batter starts to swing at a pitch, but attempts to hold up before his bat crosses over the plate, resulting in a call one way or the other by an Umpire.

Check swing, did he go?, yes he did!

Chest High/Letters High

Meaning: A pitch that crosses the plate just above the strike zone, about the height of the team-name lettering on the Batter's jersey.

And that pitch is letters high, above the zone, for ball four, and Taylor takes first base on a walk.

Chin Music

Meaning: A fastball pitch that is high and tight, forcing the Batter to move back rapidly to avoid being struck.

Carlson serves up chin music to Parker, which should have the salutary effect of moving him off the plate for the next pitch.

Choke Up

Meaning: In batting, to hold the bat handle slightly higher towards the barrel in order to enable quicker hands at the expense of sheer power.

This is a crucial at-bat for the Porcupines, and Willy Williams chokes up on the bat, needing that sac-fly to score the winning run.

Circus Catch/Miracle Catch

Meaning: A spectacular catch by a fielder, displaying exceptional athleticism and effort.

Reynoso made that circus catch, upside down and sideways, for the final out of the inning.

Clean-up Batter

Meaning: The fourth Batter in the starting lineup.

With runners at the corners, clean-up Batter Ray Ratner steps into the Batter's box with an axe to grind against head-hunter, Stan Wilmington.

Climb the Ladder

Meaning: When a Pitcher pitches higher and higher, in and out of the strike zone, to induce a swing and a miss.

The high fastball gets Upjohn to climb the ladder, and even up the count at two and two.

Climbs the Ladder

Meaning: When a Batter successfully hits a ball that was pitched high, out of the strike zone.

Espinosa climbs the ladder on that pitch and sends it into the left-center gap for a stand-up double.

Closer

Meaning: The strongest Relief Pitcher in the club, typically reserved to keep a close game close or for a save situation.

It's the top of the ninth and Closer, Ed Thorn, comes in for the save, with the Land Birds leading three to one.

Close the Book

Meaning: That point in time when the game statistics on a particular Player are set and cannot change.

The tying run is attributed to the lead-off Batter's walk, and that will close the books on Hosenozzle.

Club

Meaning: The parent team of a professional baseball organization.

The club's head office called the losing Manager in for a come-to-Jesus conversation.

Coach(es)

Meaning: On any given baseball team, these are the various persons who coach, for their team, batting, fielding, catching, bullpen, pitching, runners at first base, runners at second and third base and a "Bench Coach."

Batting Coach, Pearly Jameson, watched Simpson hit a few in the cage and had one suggestion, "Stop stepping in the bucket."

Coach's Box

Meaning: A three-sided, white-chalk lined, area in foul territory roughly adjacent to each of first and third base, as the area where, for the most part, the respective base coaches for the offensive team stand during their team's at-bats.

Smithson charged toward third, with Coach Himelsocker down the baseline, well outside the coach's box, emphatically signally the green light to run home.

The **Collar/Took the Collar** (*see also*: O-fer)

Meaning: When a Player fails to get any hits in the game and he is "O-fer."

In the tenth game in a row taking the collar, Buncy sauntered back to his dugout.

Come-backer

Meaning: A ball hit by a Batter directly back toward the pitching mound.

Oh, and Crow snagged that come-backer with a back-hand glove for the third out of the inning.

Command/In the Zone

Meaning: When a Pitcher has exceptionally good control of his pitches in and outside of the strike zone.

Olivera has been in the zone in this outing, with twelve Ks, one walk and one hit over the seventeen Batters he's faced.

Contact Hitter

Meaning: A hitter who is not particularly known for his power as a hitter, but frequently makes effective contact with the ball for situational hitting.

Mendoza, one of the finest contact hitters in the Majors, sent a line drive to left-center field to score the winning run from second base.

Corked Bat

Meaning: A bat which has been illegally altered by drilling the barrel and replacing wood core with cork, then capping it off, to enhance the rebound effect on a batted ball.

The League Office suspended Slugger Willy McPeters for ten games following his corked bat exploding on contact in a game against the Belmont Bombers.

The Count

Meaning: At any particular time during an at-bat, the number of balls and strikes attributed to the Batter, with the balls represented first and the strikes represented last. For example, 2 balls and 1 strike would be a 2-1 count.

Bases loaded, the count's three an' two, and the payoff pitch is…a ball; they walked him, and just walked in the tying run.

Country Mile

Meaning: A long-ways, with a wide margin for error.

Despite a good jump and powerful stride, Paul D. Jameson was out at second by a country mile, off the rocket throw by Catcher Jack Fleischli.

Cover (a base)

Meaning: For a defensive Player to set up at a base, ready for a throw to force or tag out a baserunner.

As Usain laid down a perfect bunt, Shortstop Paladin covered third.

Crew Chief

Meaning: This is the Umpire, within the umpiring crew at a baseball game, who has the *most seniority* within that crew, and is charged with the responsibility for leadership and overall supervision of the umpiring crew for that particular game.

Crew Chief Bart Sadler ended the brouhaha by ejecting the vociferous Manager, Wiley Baxter, from the ballgame.

Crooked Number(s)

Meaning: Any number of runs, more than one, scored in a single inning.

It was a sad day in Millville, with the Rangers posting crooked numbers in every one of the first four innings.

Crowding the Plate

Meaning: Where a hitter sets up in the Batter's box closer than usual to home plate, in order to be better able to reach pitches outside of the normal strike zone.

Futterman makes a practice of crowding the plate but Spangler will have none of it and throws a heater, high and tight.

Crow Hop

Meaning: Footwork utilized by any position Player upon fielding the ball, to create forward momentum and to create a stable platform on landing, so as to improve both the speed and accuracy of the throw.

Underhill fielded the ground ball well, but instead of moving into a crow hop, he threw to first in a somewhat static and off-balance stance, the throw was short and the Stars First-baseman was unable come up with the ball.

Curve/Curve Ball/Breaking Ball/Bender

Meaning: A medium speed pitch thrown with such rotation as to cause the flight toward the plate to be elliptical.

> *Stricklin is known as a fastball-slider Pitcher but his curve ball baffled Williams for strike three, to end the top of the inning.*

Cut-off/Cut/Take the Cut (verb)

Meaning: When a ball is batted to the outfield, this is the act of receiving a throw prior to its ultimate destination, creating an option of whether and where to throw the ball next in the play.

> *Patterson takes the cut from right field, throws a strike to Jordy Jackson to gun down the runner at second—but a run scores.*

Cut-off Man/Cut-off/Cut (noun)

Meaning: The defensive Player, in the particular situation, to whom a cut-off throw is to be thrown.

> *Third-baseman, Winston Featherman, sets up for the cut but Appleton's throw from left is air-mailed over the cut-off man and over the Catcher, allowing the run to score.*

Cutter

Meaning: A version of a 4-seam fastball pitch, thrown with two fingers evenly across a seam, thumb tucked under, wrist firm and delivery with the two fingers *slightly to the outside*, producing a combination backspin and gyro and causing the ball to "cut" horizontally a few inches to the Pitcher's glove side as it nears the plate.

> *Edenberry had command of a four-seamer, change, slider and cutter, but never had much luck with a split-finger fastball.*

D

Dead Ball

Meaning: A ball that is no longer in play—for example a foul ball off of a Batter's body, a balk, hit by pitch, spectator interference · and interference with a fielder's right of way.

As soon as the spectator touched the ball on the fly in fair territory, it was a dead ball and ruled a ground-rule double.

Deep in the Count

Meaning: a full count or close to a full count for the Batter.

Gunderson choked up on the bat, deep in the count, trying for that ground ball behind the runner.

Delivery

Meaning: The particular style and mechanics of a given Pitcher's pitch.

Vernon's delivery was somewhat unorthodox, but for a sixteen-year-old, he showed real promise as a powerful Pitcher.

Designated Hitter/DH

Meaning: The non-mandatory use of a Batter in place of any player (almost always, the Pitcher) has become standard throughout the Majors, and typically would bat anywhere in the batting order in the discretion of that team's Manager.

It is now almost universally accepted that the DH system is much more exciting than requiring Pitchers to hit.

Deuces Wild

Meaning: When there's two baserunners on base, with two outs, and a count of two balls and two strikes on the Batter.

Pacino evens up the count and it's deuces wild with the tying run at the plate.

Diamond/Baseball Field/Baseball Diamond

Meaning: The playing field in a baseball game, oriented with home plate and second base aligned to center field.

Veracruz walked out onto the diamond, taking it all in, at 11:43 p.m. the night before his first game in the Majors.

Dig In

Meaning: When a Batter turns his cleats back and forth in the Batter's box dirt to get a firm footing for a hard-hitting swing.

Yancy was anything but pleased to see Miranda digging in at the plate, and threw chin music to return the favor.

Disabled List/DL

Meaning: A list of varying lengths of time, onto which are placed Players too injured to play for the time being and considered to then be off of the 40-man roster.

Owen Underhill was placed on the 10-day DL when his sore big toe flared up, again.

Dish/Home Plate/Plate/Platter/Home

Meaning: A hard-rubber square, with a triangular side facing the Pitcher, over which a pitch must be pitched in order to be considered a strike and onto which a baserunner from third base must eventually contact in order to score a run.

From the way Home Plate Umpire Burt Bennington was calling balls and strikes, you'd think the platter was half its regulation size.

Dive/Dives

Meaning: Similar to a feet-first slide except the baserunner goes to the ground *head-first* into the bag he is approaching.

Hornsby dives into the bag at third and the call is…safe!

Doctoring the Ball

Meaning: Illegally scuffing or applying a foreign substance to a baseball in a game.

Pitcher Yank McQueen was notorious for doctoring the ball and this time, the Umpire had him dead to rights.

Donut

Meaning: A donut-shaped weight, placed over the bat handle and lodged against the barrel of the bat, used by an on-deck Batter to temporarily add weight to the barrel of his bat, to help him loosen up his arms in anticipation of the at-bat.

Remington grabbed the donut and warmed up, all the while going to school on Smither's delivery.

Double/Two-bagger

Meaning: A situation in which the Batter safely reaches second base, from a batted ball, not the result of a fielding error or fielder's choice.

Headly Vestermark just ripped a frozen rope to the right-center field gap for a two-bagger.

Double Header/Twin Bill

Meaning: Where two teams play each other in two separate games on the same day, typically occurring to make up for a previously canceled game due to some cause such as a rain-out.

The Phoenix Bulldogs and Pittsburg Centurions face off today in a Double Header that could stretch each of their respective bullpens to the breaking point.

Double Play

Meaning: With at least one baserunner already on base, where the defensive team is able to make two outs during the course of one batted ball, such as the classic 6-4-3 combination (Shortstop to Second-baseman to First-baseman).

The inning was closed out, and the Baltimore lead preserved, with the double play of Cartwright to Blinky to Zack.

Double Steal

Meaning: Where two baserunners, on a play usually called or otherwise signaled by the Third Base Coach, attempt a simultaneous steal of their next respective bases, typically first to second and second to third.

> *Third Base Coach flashed his signs, Batter Steven Indigo takes a slow curve and Ballantine and Rippley are off to the races in a double steal.*

Double Up

Meaning: When a fielder catches a fly ball and throws out a baserunner before he can return to the bag he had been on prior to the flyball having been hit.

> *Perkins snags a frozen rope to third base and doubles up Vestermark at first.*

Down Broadway/Down the Chute/Down the Pipe

Meaning: A fastball thrown right through the heart of the plate.

> *With an exit velocity of 120 miles an hour, Pennypacker went yard off a four-seam fastball down Broadway.*

Downstairs/Low

Meaning: A pitch crossing the plate below the strike zone.

> *Count even at two and two, Ventura into his windup and it is...downstairs for ball three.*

Down Swinging

Meaning: For a Batter to strike out swinging at and missing the pitch, or foul-tipping the ball into the Catcher's mitt, for a third strike.

> *Edinger goes down swinging and that is the eighth strikeout for the Crazy-Eights' Pitcher, Dwight "Goodnight" Jones.*

Drag Bunt

Meaning: Used mostly but not exclusively by hitters who bat left, this is a last moment bunt for an attempted single, where the Batter coordinates his bat placement with physically moving toward first base.

> *Lefty Gomez executed the perfect drag bunt up the first base line, and narrowly beat out the Pitcher's throw.*

Draw a Walk

Meaning: When a Batter earns a walk by the Pitcher throwing four called-balls without the Batter hitting the ball into fair territory, hitting a foul ball that is caught on the fly, or getting three strikes.

> *Mighty Joe Watkins was a notorious long-ball hitter, but on this at-bat, he drew a walk.*

Drive in a Run

Meaning: Where an RBI, other than the Batter himself, is credited to a Batter.

In the bottom of the ninth, with a runner on second and the score tied, Severson drove in the winning run with a line shot to right-center field.

Drop Off the Table/Falls Off the Table

Meaning: Any pitch that takes a nasty drop downward just before crossing, or passing through, the strike zone.

Shortstop, Ronald Johnson, fanned air for strike three as he swung at a vicious forkball that fell off the table.

Dropped Third Strike

Meaning: If a pitch, which would be the third strike to a Batter, is dropped by the Catcher, the Batter may attempt to reach first base safely before either being tagged out or the ball is caught by a fielder (almost always the First-baseman) who is in contact with the first base bag.

Jock Wilson swung and missed the cutter, and when Clancy dropped the third strike, Wilson broke for first but was swiftly tagged out.

Drop-weight

Meaning: The positive or negative value of the weight of a bat in ounces versus the length of a bat in inches, such that, for example, a 33-inch bat weighing 30 ounces has a drop-weight of -3.

Jack's handcrafted, pro-grade, well-balanced maple bat had the maximum allowable drop-weight of -3, and man was it a doosey.

Ducks on the Pond

Meaning: Two or three baserunners on base, when the next Batter comes to bat.

From the Tigers dugout, as Perkins stepped into the Batter's box, Sepulveda yelled out, "Whatayasay Perks, ducks on the pond, ducks on the pond!"

Dugout

Meaning: The somewhat-exposed area in which staff, and Players not on the playing field, wait, prepare for their at-bats and watch the ball game when not fielding or hitting.

Manager Sly Abbot made sure that by game time, there was always plenty of bubble gum in the dugout for the Players.

Dusted Off

Meaning: When a ball is pitched close to the head of the Batter, to stop him from crowding the plate.

Billy Wilson was trying to take one for the team, but instead, was dusted off.

Earned Run

Meaning: Any run attributable to a Pitcher's stats—*i.e.*, where the baserunner initially reached base while the particular Pitcher was in the game, and the run did not result from a passed ball or fielding error.

When it was in the books on Ireland, he'd worked five and a third innings with two earned runs.

Earned Run Average/ERA

Meaning: The average number of earned runs attributable to a Pitcher projected into 9-inning games. For example, the Pitcher pitches 5 innings and has 2 runs counted as earned runs attributable to his pitching outing. Divide 2 runs by 5 innings and multiply by 9 innings equals a 3.6 ERA for that game for that Pitcher.

Westerfield's season ERA was a remarkable 1.75.

Eephus Pitch

Meaning: A rare pitch in baseball which is slow and with a high arc, and surprisingly difficult for baseball Players to hit.

With the game completely out of reach, the Sharks Manager moved their Shortstop to the mound, who proceeded to throw his Eephus pitch.

Emery Ball/Scuff Ball

Meaning: A baseball rendered illegal from surface alterations intended to affect the movement of pitches.

Hammerin' Hugh Edmonton had a knack of throwin' scuff balls, and some say he marked 'em with his belt buckle.

Error

Meaning: A fielding play, resulting in a hitter reaching a base or any baserunner advancing one or more bases, which the official scorer determines could have been prevented by ordinary defensive effort at the particular level of baseball (such as Major League Baseball) being played.

Pineapple James was as reliable as any at second base, but in this game, he already had two errors and counting.

Everyday Player

Meaning: Not only on the 40-man roster but a position player, who appears regularly in his team's starting lineup.

Tarkington wanted to be an everyday Player, and worked hard to achieve that goal, but for now, he was considered to be a pinch hitter and back-up utility Player.

Extra Base Hit(s)

Meaning: Any hit more than a single, typically referring to a double or a triple.

Virgil swatted the ball down the third baseline, past Taggert at third and into left field for an extra base hit.

Extra Innings

Meaning: Additional innings as necessitated by a tie after the completion of a regulation number of innings.

After nine complete innings, the Philadelphia Squirrels and the Los Angeles Labradors are tied at 7-7, and we're headed into extra innings.

F

Fair Ball/Fair

Meaning: A batted ball which is touched by a defensive Player on or inside the foul lines, or comes to rest on or inside the foul lines, or bounces on or inside a foul line and stays on or inside the foul line while passing over or touching first or third bases, or lands on the playing field beyond first or third base and on or inside the foul lines, or leaves the field of play on the fly touching or inside the foul poles in left or right fields (home runs).

> *It's got the distance, and if it's a fair ball, it's a home run and it is…foul.*

Fair Territory

Meaning: Generally, any area of the playing field that is on or inside either of the foul lines, including any portion of the bases and the foul poles in left and right field.

> *Carlucci can slap that ball anywhere in fair territory and no one knows where he's going next.*

Farm Team/Minors

Meaning: The various levels of professional training teams which each Major League team owns and operates as a source of trades and potential Major League Players.

> *Pickering was drafted by the Boilers out of college in 2012, and worked his way through the Minors until brought up in 2015.*

Fastball/Heater/Gas/Heat/Burner/Heater/Cheese

Meaning: A ball that may have some movement, but is primarily effective against a hitter for its inherent speed to and across the plate.

Appleman's average was a respectable .298, but he goes down swinging on a burner for strike three.

Feed

Meaning: A careful throw or soft toss by one fielder to another to enable him to make an out and, as possible, to turn a double play.

Westerfeld receives the feed from Second-baseman, Bob Rossi, and rockets *the ball to first for a bang-bang double play.*

Fielder

Meaning: A Player on defense, other than the Pitcher and Catcher.

With slugger Barney Tibblesacker up to bat, the Outlaws fielders were all chomping at the bit.

Fielder's Choice

Meaning: A play in which the defensive Players ignore the Batter in order to make the out at second, third or home, in which case the at-bat does not result in a "hit" being scored in favor of the Batter, unless the Official Scorer determines, in his or her sound discretion, that the fielder did not have a chance to retire the Batter.

Upton hit into a fielder's choice, the runner advancing to second is out and the Eagles are now down to their last out in the bottom of the ninth.

Field the Ball

Meaning: For a fielder to catch a batted ball.

A sharp hit to left-center field, and Marshak fields the ball, fires it past the cut to home plate and the runner is...tagged out by Rubio.

Fighting Off (a pitch)

Meaning: Especially with two strikes on a Batter, and facing a difficult strike to make solid contact, the Batter just tries to foul it off to avoid striking out, and to get a better pitch to hit or possibly to earn a walk.

A four-seamer at 94 miles an hour, and Clemens is forced to fight it off with a foul ball up to the third deck behind home plate.

Find the Handle

Meaning: Inability of a fielder to cleanly catch a batted ball, typically resulting in the Batter arriving safely at first base or a baserunner advancing.

On what appeared to be a routine grounder to short, Morgan just couldn't find the handle and all runners are safe; bases now loaded.

First Base/First

Meaning: The bag 90 feet to the right of home plate, first in a sequence of four, counting home plate.

The nubber dribbled toward first base, and finally came to a rest inside the baseline, for a hit.

First-baseman

Meaning: The Player assigned, on defense, to the infield position in the first base area.

First-baseman, Bill Fairchild, was a three-time Platinum Glove at his position, and was known to his teammates as The Vacuum.

First-baseman's Mitt

Meaning: A leather, relatively long, fielding mitt, without open finger slots, particularly designed for the First-baseman in catching and scooping balls thrown by other players.

After the last out, Scanlan hustled to the grandstands, handing his First-baseman's mitt to the wheelchair-bound young boy who had been so encouraging throughout the game.

Flag Down

Meaning: For a fielder to catch or knock down a frozen rope.

That ball was ripped down the line and barely flagged down by Third-baseman Paul Taggert for the third out.

Flip

Meaning: An often-discouraged practice drill (because of Player-safety concerns) where several baseball Players form a circle and flip and catch the ball using only their gloves.

The Skip turned a blind eye to their game of flip, knowing how those skills come in handy in a game situation.

Fly Ball

Meaning: A batted ball high in the air, generally to the outfield, which may or may not be in fair territory.

On the run in a circus catch, Jones picked off that fly ball in foul territory for the last out of the inning.

Fly Out

Meaning: When a fly ball is caught on the fly by a fielder.

That ball is way back there and…a fly out, caught by Stanley in center.

Force

Meaning: When baserunners must progress to the next base on a fair ball, a walk or a hit by pitch.

Parsons, the original baserunner at second, apparently forgot that he was in a force situation and was tagged out when Slatkin arrived at second.

Force Out

Meaning: When a fielder in control of the ball touches a bag prior to a runner, who is forced to advance, touching the bag, or prior to a tagging up runner tagging up on the bag, in which case, the runner is out.

Zander fields the ball cleanly at Short and feeds Toyo at second for the force out.

Force-play

Meaning: Any defensive play which, if successful, results in a force out.

They have a force-play at third and Quigley dives toward the bag to beat the runner and…gets the out!

Forkball

Meaning: A type of pitch thrown with the Pitcher's fingers spread widely on the ball, causing the pitch to drop radically before reaching the strike zone.

The Nashville Firemen have had trouble all night with Yamashiro's forkball, and this at-bat by powerhouse hitter, Dale Martin, is no exception.

Foul Ball

Meaning: Any batted ball that is not a fair ball.

Edwards has now hit seven, count 'em, seven foul balls in this at-bat, running up the pitch count for Nate Fendermeister to thirty-six in the first inning.

Foul Lines

Meaning: Straight, white-chalk lines extending, 90 degrees from each other, on the field from the home plate to the outfield fence, outside of which lines is foul territory and on or inside of which lines is fair territory.

Clancy keeps hitting hard shots but they're all headed outside the foul lines and you just know he wants to straighten one of those babies out.

Foul Off/Stay Alive

Meaning: For a Batter to hit a pitched ball into foul territory, sometimes intentionally to stay alive for further pitches. *See,* Fighting Off.

Tac Peterson's at-bat is a good one, staying alive through fouling off ball after ball.

Foul Out

Meaning: A ball batted into foul territory and caught on the fly by a defensive Player.

Young hits a towering fly ball into left field, slicing foul; Masters tracks it down and it's a foul out in the top of the fourth.

Foul Poles

Meaning: Vertical poles, and inside screens, extending vertically from the outfield ends of the respective left field and right field foul lines, outside of which on the fly is a foul, and touching or inside of which on the fly is a hit and if above the wall, a home run.

Hendrix hit a blistering shot to right field which rebounded on the fly off of the foul pole just below the top of the outfield wall, for a stand-up triple.

Foul Territory/Foul Ground

Meaning: Anything outside of the foul lines and foul poles.

Porter's bunt rolled slowly into foul territory, where Sanchez quickly snatched it up.

Foul Tip (caught by Catcher)

Meaning: A batted ball fouled directly into the Catcher's glove and *caught*, resulting in a strike, even if it is the third strike, and during which baserunners *are permitted* to attempt to advance, at their own risk, without tagging up.

A hit and run was on, but when Ellis foul tipped, Elroy rocketed the ball to second for a strike him out, throw him out.

Foul Tip (dropped by Catcher)

Meaning: A batted ball fouled directly into the Catcher's glove but *dropped*, resulting in a mere foul ball, and thus, not a strike if it would be the third strike, and during which baserunners are not permitted to attempt to advance without tagging up.

Full count on Ripley, foul-tipped but Montecito drops the ball—still full count—and the baserunners return to their respective bases.

Four-seam Fastball/Four-seamer

Meaning: A fast pitch that unleashes all of the Pitcher's power for pure speed. The four-seamer is thrown by gripping the ball with the index and middle fingers fully across the looping-shaped seams of the baseball, with the thumb underneath for stability and balance. In an over-the-top release, the fingers roll over the seams, creating backspin.

The West Siders' closer was well known for his 105 miles an hour, four-seamer, and this outing would be no exception.

Frame a Pitch

Meaning: The act of a Catcher in positioning his body and/ or his Catcher's mitt for a particular pitch that will be or has been thrown, particularly to portray the pitch to the Umpire as having crossed the plate within the strike zone; and for a Pitcher, to pitch a ball intentionally to a particular part of the strike zone.

Let me tell you this—framing a pitch on the changeup is not an easy thing to do.

Frozen Pizza

Meaning: When a Batter with two strikes expects one type of pitch, is surprised by the actual pitch and takes the pitch for a third strike.

When asked about his strikeout-looking in the fifth, Jenner explained, that with two strikes, he expected a breaking ball and instead got a frozen pizza.

Frozen Rope/Rope/Line Drive/Liner

Meaning: A batted ball that is hit hard, fair or foul, with a low trajectory.

Oh, and it's a rocket shot, a frozen rope, to right field and Billy Marconi will score the go-ahead run!

Full House/Full Count/Full Boat/Count is Full

Meaning: When the count on a Batter is three balls and two strikes.

Folks, it doesn't get better than this, in the bottom of the ninth, two outs, bases loaded, the home team down by three, and a full count on "The Jack Attack" Forbes at the plate.

Fungo/Fungo Bat

Meaning: A specialized, lightweight, slender bat, used for hitting practice balls to fielders.

Coach Maxwell was hitting fungo shots to outfielders, who one-by-one scrambled to catch the fly balls.

G

Gap/Alley/Power Alley

Meaning: The outfield areas between left field and center, and between center field and right.

Mooney's shot deep to the left-center gap should score Chris Hutchinson from first base, and with his speed on the basepaths, it does just that.

Game Ball/Ball

Meaning: The particular baseball which is in play at any given time in a baseball game.

To the surprise of everyone, Denton's wild pitch caused the game ball to become wedged between boards in the backstop.

Gapper/Gap Shot

Meaning: A batted ball hit into one of the gaps.

That gapper will score Tommy Parks, and Wheeler arrives at second in a stand-up double.

Get a Good Piece of It

Meaning: Often used to describe hitting the ball well in a successful hit.

Yuker got a good piece of that screwball and he'll arrive safely at first, 2 for 3 on the night.

Get on (one's) Horse

Meaning: For a Player, typically an outfielder, to run at top speed to field a batted ball.

Jimanez really has to get on his horse for that one and he... makes a spectacular catch!

Getting Shelled

Meaning: Where a Pitcher is giving up a lot of hits and runs to an opposing team.

The Brooklyn hurler is really getting shelled tonight and it just does not seem likely that he'll make it out of the fifth inning.

Glove/Mitt

Meaning: The shaped, laced and padded leather covering used by baseball Players on defense to help them catch a batted or thrown ball, or, in the case of a Pitcher, to also shield his grip on the ball from the Batter's view.

Cunningham manipulated the ball within his glove and was ready to throw his very deceptive split-finger fastball.

Go-ahead run

Meaning: The baserunner or run which takes or would take the offensive team into the lead.

Taylor's up to bat with the go-ahead run in scoring position at second.

Go Down in Order/Three Up, Three Down

Meaning: When, during a team's half-inning on offense, the first three Batters are retired on outs.

For the Jaguars, it was three up, three down as they went down in order to close out the seventh inning.

Going Around/Went Around

Meaning: When a strike occurs, not as a called strike or a full swing strike, but because in what would otherwise have been a called ball, the Plate Umpire spontaneously, or on request, a baseline Umpire, determines that the Batter's bat crossed over the plate before being pulled back by the Batter.

Did he go around?—yes he did!

Golden Sombrero

Meaning: A light-hearted jab whenever a Player strikes out four times within a single game.

And with that whiff, Whittaker gets the Golden Sombrero for today's performance at the plate.

Gold Glove/Rawlings Golden Glove Award

Meaning: A prestigious defensive, gold-lamé-leather glove trophy awarded by Rawlings each year to Players in each fielding position, including a utility Player, and a team award in each of the American and National Leagues of Major League Baseball, as determined from metrics and by the vote of managers and coaches of each league (who may not vote for their own Players), and including some softball-related awards as well.

My high school friend, Bobby Grich, earned four Gold Glove awards in 1973, 1974, 1975 and 1976 from his outstanding defensive performance at second base.

Good Eye

Meaning: Describing a Batter who can lay off a pitch or pitches outside the strike zone.

Young Jackie had a surprisingly good eye at the plate, especially considering that he was near-sighted.

Good Face

Meaning: A baseball scout's vision of a top prospect's look: athletic, square jaw, forceful, extrovert, confident, piercing eyes that show strength, energy, and a feeling of calm aggression and eloquence with solid eye contact.

That new kid's got a good face, with a coordinated, muscular physique.

Good morning, good afternoon, good night

Meaning: When a Pitcher faces and retires the first three Batters of any given half-inning.

It was good morning, good afternoon and good night for the Buzzards in the top of the eighth inning.

Good Take

Meaning: When a Batter doesn't swing the bat at a pitched ball that is not within the strike zone.

Attaboy Sammy, righteous good take on a nasty cutter.

Got 'Em Guessing

Meaning: When the Pitcher has the Batter confused as to what pitch is coming up next.

Yardley is outstanding today with six Ks in the first three innings and he's really got 'em guessing.

Go the Distance

Meaning: To pitch until the regulation innings have been completed.

Xander has never gone past 115 pitches but at this pace he just might go the distance.

Got Him

Meaning: When a Pitcher manages to get a Batter out, typically on strikes.

Here's the payoff pitch and...got him!

Go Yard/Jack it Out/Jack One Out/Take Him Deep (verb)

Meaning: To hit a home run.

He's had a ten game slump in home runs and you just know Carlos has bad intentions to jack one out.

Grand Slam/Granny/Salami

Meaning: A home run with baserunners on all three bases.

The tying run at the plate, down six-two and…Landis blasts it to center, going long and…a grand slam for Steve Landis, only the second in his Big League career!

The Great Seats

Meaning: A light-hearted expression for spectator seats located very high up in the stadium.

Well, kids, it's not field level, but we're in the Great Seats with hot dogs, peanuts, sodas and perfect weather, and it should be an awesome game.

Green Light

Meaning: When a hitter is given permission to swing at will on a 3 balls/no strikes count, or a runner is given permission to attempt to steal a base at will.

Bennington's a contact hitter, and with a runner in scoring position and one out, he's got a green light to hit it hard anywhere he can.

Ground Ball/Grounder

Meaning: A pitched ball that is hit by a Batter and bounces at least once in the infield.

And Ramos hits a routine grounder to second, which Toomey scoops up, tosses to first for the out.

Ground Out (noun)/Grounds Out (verb),

Meaning: When a Batter hits a ground ball, which is fielded, and the Batter is thrown out in a force play at first base.

Rivera grounds out for the out-number-two, and Craig Peterman steps into the box.

Ground-rule Double/Automatic Double

Meaning: A ball, hit fairly, but which somehow goes out of play, and according to the ground rules is deemed a double

That ball was well-hit to the right-center gap, and over the wall on one bounce for a ground-rule double.

Gun Down

Meaning: For a Player to throw the ball, where the fielder receiving it successfully tags out the runner.

Edwards takes the bounce off the wall, crow-hops and he... guns down Bishop at second.

H

Half (of the inning)/Top Half of the Inning/ Top of the Inning/Bottom Half of the Inning/Bottom of the Inning/Frame

Meaning: An inning is comprised of the top half (or, "top") of the inning when the visiting team bats, and the bottom half (or, "bottom") of the inning when the home team bats (unless leading after the top of the ninth inning in which case the game is over). Each half of an inning is also known as a frame.

Leading off in the bottom of the third inning is Zinter, followed by Oliver and Painter.

Hammer

Meaning: When a Batter hits the ball very hard.

Pitched up, but Smithers hammers that ball which takes a high bounce into left field for a single.

Handcuff

Meaning: Pitch to a Batter inside so that the Batter cannot extend his arms during a swing.

Young was handcuffed on that pitch, hits a slow-roller to third and…beats the throw to first.

Handle

Meaning: A firm and reliable grip on the ball to allow a solid throw.

It was a hard-hit grounder to Landers but he just couldn't get a handle on the ball and Munoz arrives at first base on an error.

Hands Like Frying Pans/Hard Hands

Meaning: A fielder's tendency to be clumsy and prone to errors in catching balls.

If Reynoso weren't a three-hundred hitter, he couldn't play in Single A with those hands like frying pans.

Hanging (a Pitch)/**Hanging Curve**

Meaning: Pitching a ball, particularly a curveball, which instead of breaking toward the corners or out of the strike zone, breaks neatly into the heart of the plate in a perfect spot for the Batter.

Banks spotted that hanging curve and went yard with ducks on the pond.

Hardball/Baseball

Meaning: The game, distinguished from softball, using a smaller, more compact ball, overhand pitching, a larger field of play and permitting lead-offs, for example.

Out of college I played some slow-pitch softball, but starting in my early 30s, I went back to hardball in open leagues for thirteen years.

Hat Trick

Meaning: A joking or disparaging term for when a Player strikes out three times in a single game. But also used as a compliment for a Player who hits three home runs in a single game.

Peterson takes strike three to earn himself a hat trick for the day, so far.

Headhunter

Meaning: A disparaging term describing a Pitcher with a reputation of throwing beanballs.

That Percy Simmons was a headhunter was a well-known fact; but whether he would be ejected by tonight's no-nonsense Home Plate Umpire, Rodrigo Domingo San Diego Gonzales, remained to be seen.

Heart of the Plate

Meaning: The very center of the strike zone over the plate.

With a three-two count, the Pitcher wants to hit a corner and stay away from the heart of the plate.

Hidden Ball Trick

Meaning: A play where a baseman conceals a ball in play and waits for the baserunner at his base to step off the bag, at which moment the baseman can tag him out.

Park never threw the ball back, the coaches weren't looking, everyone thinks Danny's got the ball on the mound and... Park tags out the baserunner in a brilliant hidden ball trick.

High and Tight

Meaning: A pitch thrown at or above the letters and inside.

Timmons is known for his high and tight pitches and I think a low and away slider is coming next.

High Cheese/High Heat

Meaning: A fastball pitched high in the strike zone.

Penrose climbed the ladder, knocks that high cheese and it is way gone.

Hit

Meaning: A hit is a batted ball in fair territory which results in the Batter reaching at least first base safely, and not as a result of a fielder's choice or error.

That closes the books on Charlie, who has five strikeouts, three walks, four hits and has given up two earned runs.

Hit and Run

Meaning: When a coach signals both the Batter and baserunner(s) that on the next pitch, the Batter will swing to hit the ball behind the Baserunner, and the Baserunner will take off toward his next base.

With Gonzales on first, the hit and run was on and Bustamonte hit a rocket ground ball out to right field, advancing the runner and putting two men aboard.

Hit Away

Meaning: Often following a failed attempted bunt, a coach's sign to the Batter that he is free to make a normal swing at the following pitch.

With a 3 and 1 count, Sanders will hit away.

Hit Behind the Runner

Meaning: With less than two outs, for a Batter to attempt to hit the ball to the right side of the infield, to enable a baserunner or baserunners to advance station to station.

Butler hit behind the runner perfectly, who moved into scoring position with two outs.

Hit by Pitch/HBP

Meaning: A Batter is awarded first base if during his at-bat, he is unable, with reasonable effort, to avoid being struck to any part of his body or clothing by a pitched ball.

More than any other Player this year in the Majors, Jimmy Swindel has more hit by pitch credits than any other active Player, and it happened again tonight for number twenty-four.

Hitch in One's Swing

Meaning: Generally, a bad hitting habit where, as a pitch is released, the Batter moves his bat significantly *backwards*, before moving it forward in a swing.

Early in the season, Joe Jennings had a brutal hitch in his swing, but in the last fourteen games, and with help from batting coach Chris Gautschi, he's corrected that bad habit, and with excellent results.

Hit for the Cycle

Meaning: When, in a single game, a Batter collects at least one each of a single, a double, a triple and a home run.

Reynolds slams one to the right-field gap for a stand-up double, and for the second time in his career, he hit for the cycle!

Hit for the Natural Cycle

Meaning: When in a single game, a Batter hits a single, a double, a triple and a home run, *in that precise sequence.*

Folks, this is so rare, most people have never even heard of it, but with that home run, Jimmy Winters of the Baltimore Peacocks has just hit for the natural cycle!

Hit for the Home Run Cycle

Meaning: When, in a single game, a Batter hits at least one each of a solo home run, a two-run home run, a three-run home run and a grand slam. (*Note*, there is no hitting for a "*natural* home run cycle" since it is only hypothetical and has *never* to date been known to have occurred in an actual baseball game at any level)

Tonight, Burt Bee of the Toledo Tornados made Major League history, as he hit for the home run cycle!

Hit Parade

Meaning: A series of several hits by one team in the same inning.

Relief Pitcher, Humberto Ubertino, had no control, no speed and no game plan, and served up a hit parade to the Razorbacks in the bottom of the eighth inning.

Hit the Deck

Meaning: When a Batter is compelled to drop to the dirt to avoid being hit by a pitched ball.

Stevens tried to hit the deck but the high and tight fastball managed to drill him in his left shoulder.

Hit the Wall

Meaning: When a Pitcher is so exhausted from a high pitch count that he can no longer pitch effectively.

Peters pitched five and a third innings but hit the wall after his 97th pitch.

Hitter's Count

Meaning: A balls and strike count where the Batter has a significant advantage over the Pitcher.

Artemus had a hitter's count at two and "oh" and was sitting on a fastball down Broadway.

Hold

Meaning: When a Relief Pitcher enters the game in a save situation, gets at least one out and leaves the game without finishing the game and without giving up the lead. However, a Relief Pitcher cannot leave a game until he faces at least three batters, unless he is injured or completes an inning.

Carter earns a "hold" for that performance and the game remains Bulldogs five, Renegades four.

Hold the Runner

Meaning: Cooperation taking place between the Pitcher (looking over prior to the next pitch) and the First-baseman camping out at or very near first base, to prevent the Runner from taking a large lead-off.

With the game on the line and the tying run on first, Martin's first order of business was to hold the runner.

Hold Up on a Swing/Checked (One's) Swing (verb)

Meaning: After starting to swing at a pitch which would otherwise be called a ball, and the Batter decides not to swing and is able to prevent the barrel of the bat from contacting the ball or sufficiently passing across the plate.

The Plate Umpire called a strike, but only because Taylor was NOT able to hold up on his swing.

Home Game

Meaning: A game for the team whose home ballpark is the site for the game.

It's a home game tonight for the Lancaster Scorpions, in the first of a four-game homestand with the Santa Clarita Tumbleweeds.

Home Plate Umpire/Plate Umpire

Meaning: The Umpire stationed behind the Catcher and assigned to call balls and strikes, among other responsibilities.

The Plate Umpire just ejected Batter Tommy Edwards for taking exception with that horrendous called strike.

Home Run/Jack/Dinger/Yard/Moon Shot/Tater/Homer/ Round-tripper/Bomb/No Doubter/Goner/Way Gone/ Long Ball/Long Gone/Shot/Downtown/Gone/Out of the Park/*See* Ya!/Four-bagger/Quadruple/Yak/Yiketty Yak/Four-bagger/Dong/Blast (noun, adjective)

Meaning: If a Batter's hit goes on the fly over the outfield fence in fair territory.

Warner gets all of that one and it is way gone!

Home Run-in-an-Elevator/Home Run in a Silo

Meaning: A nearly vertical and very high fly ball in the infield.

This hit is headed skyward and it's a home run in an elevator, but today, the third out of the bottom of the third inning.

Home Stand

Meaning: A series of successive home games against various opposing teams.

The lead-off Batter for the Sparrows, in this first game of a three-game home stand, is Joey Remington.

Home Team

Meaning: The team whose home ballpark is the site for the game, and which bats in the bottom of the inning.

Being the home team is a slight but definite advantage, since the game is played in a familiar ballpark and since the home team always knows how its opponent has scored before it has to bat in any given inning.

Hop

Meaning: The bounce of a thrown or batted ball.

There's a one-hop to Tanzy, and a bobble, but a strong throw and the Batter is...out in a bang-bang play!

Hot Box

Meaning: The area between two fielders involved in a rundown.

Escobar is caught off base and finds himself in the hot box as he's run down by Third-baseman, Kevin Kneeler.

Hot Corner

Meaning: Another term for the third base defensive position.

Trinity's Tom Pasternack handles the hot corner as well as any ballplayer in the league.

Hung Up/Hung Out to Dry

Meaning: A baserunner who is caught off base, typically by a Pitcher's pick-off move, leading to a swift put-out or a rundown.

Vicks was off dreaming somewhere and was hung out to dry, with an easy tag out by Parker at first.

J

In a Slump

Meaning: When a Batter's success in getting hits has declined for an unusual number of games.

Whitaker's been in a slump, with a batting average over the past fifteen games now well below the Mendoza Line.

Infield

Meaning: That portion of the baseball park which comprises the diamond and the composite-dirt in fair territory around and between the bases, the plate and the base paths.

It's a routine pop fly over the infield grass and Stotsenberg has it for the second out of the second inning.

Infielder

Meaning: The First-baseman, Second-baseman, Third-baseman and Shortstop since their positions are literally in the infield, except that in implementation of the infield fly rule, the Pitcher and Catcher are also considered to be infielders.

Beatty's entire baseball career has been as an infielder, but today, inexplicably, Manager Skip Rogers has him playing in center field.

Infield Fly Rule

Meaning: A complicated rule in a situation with less than two outs, runners on first and second base, or with the bases loaded, that results in an automatic out for the Batter who has hit a pop fly, in fair territory in or about the infield, which is not caught but should have been with ordinary effort.

Under the infield fly rule, Uker's pop fly will be ruled an out, regardless of the bobble and missed catch by Second-baseman Simmons.

Infield In

Meaning: With a baserunner at third base, and a very close game in runs scored, the infield position Players, or merely first and third, might play forward from their usual defensive positions, in order to be able to stop the runner at third from scoring on a ground ball.

It's a one-one tie in the top of the ninth inning, and the Sacramento Ducks are infield in at the corners to try an' stop Carucci from scoring from third.

Inherited Runners/Inherited Baserunners

Meaning: A situation where a Relief Pitcher comes into the game in an inning where one or more baserunners are already on base.

Timmons has his hands full now, with no outs and the bases filled with inherited baserunners.

In Jeopardy

Meaning: A baserunner is subject to being put out at any time except when time is called or when overrunning first base, unless any effort is made to start toward second base.

Smith was not in jeopardy at the moment of being tagged, since time had been called.

Injured Reserve List/IL

Meaning: The list of Players who have been temporarily removed from the active roster, with a minimum required duration.

Unfortunately for the Rockets, Hausman has now been added to the IL with tendonitis in his left knee.

Inning

Meaning: The segment of a baseball game when the two opposing teams alternate on offense and defense and within which there are three outs for each team.

And after four innings, it's Convicts five, Guards seven in this charity function at the Mule River Prison.

In Scoring Position

Meaning: A baserunner at either second or third base is considered to be in scoring position since he could normally score on a base hit to the outfield, and the runner at third could normally also score, with fewer than two outs, on a sacrifice fly hit to the outfield.

With runners in scoring position, Big Jim Thompson steps into the Batter's box with his 36-inch, drop-one, piece of lumber he calls a bat.

Inside

Meaning: Describing when a pitch is out of the strike zone, to the near side, close to the Batter (as opposed to "outside," to the far side, away from the Batter).

That pitch was high and inside for ball four, loading the bases with Peter Perkins coming up to bat.

Inside the Park Home Run

Meaning: A fair ball hit which does not leave the playing field, but from which, due to unusual circumstances and without any contributing fielding errors, the Batter is able to round all of the bases and touch home plate without being tagged out.

Gatlin's got himself an inside the park home run as the outfield is still trying to chase down that illusive baseball.

Insurance Run/Insurance

Meaning: Late in the game, a run scored by the team already ahead in runs, considered to be useful in protecting the lead.

Considering that the Dragons have the top of their lineup coming up in the bottom of the ninth, that home run was a well-needed insurance run for the Sparrows.

Intentional Walk/Intentional Pass

Meaning: When a defensive team elects to allow the Batter to take first base without the necessity of their Pitcher throwing four balls.

Peterson was given an intentional pass and the bases are now loaded with one out and Kim stepping into the box.

Interference

Meaning: When a Player, spectator or Umpire (other than as an obstruction) illegally changes the course of play, intentionally or otherwise; such as when a fan reaches over the outfield fence in fair territory and catches a batted ball. *Distinguish,* Obstruction

Catcher interference was called on the field, and confirmed in review, where Schmidt's mitt touched Walker's bat on what would otherwise have been a strikeout.

In the Books

Meaning: When a game of baseball is over, it is in the books in the sense that all statistics from the game can then be determined.

And with that called strike, Madison has just thrown a perfect game which is now officially in the books.

In the Hole (adj. re: a batted ball)

Meaning: When a hit ball grounds past and between two infielders, it is considered to be in the hole.

That's in the hole for a base hit in Alvin Johnson's first at-bat in the Majors.

In the Hole (adj. re: the count on the Batter or Pitcher)

Meaning: When the count on the Batter is 3 balls and no strike, the Pitcher is in the hole; but when the count on the Batter is no balls and two strikes, the Batter is in the hole.

With Overland in the hole, Perkins will likely be sitting on a fastball.

In the Hole (noun re: sequence of batters)

Meaning: The status of being the next Batter in the lineup after the Batter who is on-deck.

Suzuki's in the hole, waiting on the steps of the dugout, bat in hand.

In the Kitchen/In His Kitchen

Meaning: A pitch that close to the Batter's hands.

That four-seamer was in the kitchen for Fleischli, but he fought it off to stay alive.

J

Jacking a Ball/Jack it Out/Jack a Homer (verb)

Meaning: To hit a home run.

Younger just jacked it out in a three-run homer for the Bobcats to take the lead, seven to six.

Jam (a Batter)

Meaning: Pitch the ball inside so as to force the Batter to swing, if at all, with his elbows bent, thereby reducing the kinetic energy applied to any hit ball.

Oh, Perkins was jammed and that ground ball will be an easy, four-three out.

Juiced

Meaning: Although it can refer to an altered baseball to make it "more lively" and capable of being hit further, the term typically refers to a Player who has used performance-enhancing drugs ("PED") which are against the rules in a baseball league.

The home run and other batting records set in the early 2000s are considered to be suspect, as they may likely have been set by juiced Players, before league-wide PED testing commenced in 2003.

Jump/Jump on the Ball

Meaning: Once a Batter swings, this is the quickness with which a defensive Player reacts to where the ball is hit, and heads to whatever position he needs to go, in order to field it.

According to stats, Quigley had one of the quickest middle-infielder jumps in all of baseball.

Junk

Meaning: Pitches that are off-speed but live—that is, having a lot of in-flight movement.

Middle-infielder, Caleb Prescott, was an effective Reliever because of his uncanny knack for throwing hard-to-hit junk.

Junkball Pitcher

Meaning: A Pitcher with a proclivity to throw junk.

Samuel Axelman was a notorious junkball Pitcher, but he did make a great living doing that for sixteen years in the Majors.

K

K

Meaning: Symbol for a strikeout, swinging.

Reliever Tommy Escobar pitched for two full innings and amassed four Ks and two fly-outs.

Backward K

Meaning: Symbol for a strikeout, looking—*i.e.*, not swinging.

In five innings of play, starter Jeremy Epstein pitched one walk, three hits, no runs, 4 Ks and 3 backward Ks.

Keep the Hitter Honest

Meaning: Mixing up the pitches to make it more difficult for the Batter to guess which category, location and speed of the pitch he is about to see.

Jeramiah Jones was a talented Pitcher last season and always kept the hitters honest through his pitch choice and sequencing.

Knock In

Meaning: The act of batting in a run and scoring an RBI.

Despite sitting out the first inning against the Bookends, Severson managed to knock in six-runs on two singles and a three-run homer.

Knock (someone) Down (verb)

Meaning: A Pitcher throwing a pitch intentionally so close to the Batter that the Batter has to drop to the ground to avoid being struck.

They didn't like all of those base hits, so next Batter up, they knocked Jacky down.

Knockdown Pitch (noun)

Meaning: A pitch that is thrown so high and tight that the Batter has to hit the deck to prevent from being struck by the pitch.

Stotsenberg collapsed like a popped balloon, barely evading Pfeifer's knockdown pitch.

Knocked Around

Meaning: When a Pitcher is ineffective and is allowing multiple base hits, usually over more than one inning.

It was only the third inning and Chino's Ace, George Landers, was getting seriously knocked around by the Tigers' Batters.

Knuckleball/Floater/Flutterball/Knuckler

Meaning: A low-velocity pitch, delivered with little or no spin, creating significant movement in its trajectory.

Trying to hit a well-thrown knuckleball is like trying to catch lightning in a bottle.

Knuckle-curve:

Meaning: A curve ball thrown as a knuckleball.

A good knuckle-curve is quite an anomaly, and if you can throw it consistently, you've got a spot pitching in the Majors.

L

Lace

Meaning: Hitting a ball between infielders, for a base hit.

Randy Reynolds just laced *that ball to right center for his* second *stand-up double of the game.*

Late Innings

Meaning: Generally speaking, the last three innings of regulation play.

In this shut out performance, Pacers Manager Burt Bingham appears happy to keep Tony Billingsly through the late innings of the game.

Launch Angle

Meaning: The angle, relative to the ground plane, starting at the point of contact with the bat, of the ball rebounding off of the hitter's bat.

Humberto tends to hit line drives...but THAT ball is way gone at a launch angle close to 40 degrees.

Lay Down/Laying Down

Meaning: Expression to describe the fact that, and the manner in which, a ball is bunted.

This may be a sacrifice bunt situation...and YES, Miguel Rodriguez lays down the perfect base hit bunt.

Lay Off/Take

Meaning: To refrain from swinging at a pitched ball, regardless of whether it is a ball or a strike, particularly if the pitch is a ball or otherwise not the kind of pitch that the Batter wants to hit.

It's a two and "O" count and Pitt lays off a slider on the corner.

Lead Off/Takes a Lead/Leading Off

Meaning: For a baserunner to step away from his base, to shorten the distance to the next base, but optimally without being so far off the bag to allow himself to be picked off.

Holden takes a lead at first and…dives back on the pick-off move by Wilmington.

Lead-off Batter

Meaning: The particular Batter in the lineup who will be the first Batter of that half of the inning.

The lead-off Batter for the Rays in the bottom of the fourth is cracker jack hitter, Randy Davis.

Lead Runner

Meaning: With multiple baserunners on base and less than two outs, the runner who is the furthest along the basepaths becomes the primary focus of the defense.

The Marlins are substituting pinch runner Jesse Henandez as their lead runner, and William Carter steps into the box.

Leaning

Meaning: A baserunner with his weight slightly shifted toward the next base.

Jeremiah McClain is leaning and … there he goes and he is… safe at second in his fourteenth steal of the season.

Left-center Gap

Meaning: The outfield area more or less centered between where the Left-fielder and the Center-fielder normally take up their positions for each pitch.

Taylor starts off the first inning with a first pitch shot to the left-center gap, sliding into to second for a double.

Left Field, Left

Meaning: The fair-territory part of the playing field comprising the outfield grass, generally to the Catcher's left, of the baseball diamond.

It's a deep pop fly to Left and Shortstop…no, Left-fielder, Paul McNearney, makes the catch to end the inning.

Left-fielder

Meaning: The outfielder whose position is basically in the outfield grass, generally to the left side of the baseball diamond.

They're on a collision course but Left-fielder Beamon ducks out of the way and Center-fielder Augusto makes a running catch.

Left-handed Bat/Right-handed Bat/Bats Left/Bats Right/Left-handed Batter/Right-handed Batter

Meaning: Describes the Batter, not the bat; such that a Batter whose right arm is away from the mound, when the Batter is in the Batter's box, is considered to be a Right-handed Batter or a Right-handed Bat, and *vice versa*.

Shortstop Huel Carson throws right but bats left.

Left On Base/LOB/Stranded

Meaning: Runners who were on base and did not score when their half of the inning is completed.

The Penguins cannot seem to get hits with runners in scoring position, are down two runs through the seventh inning and have stranded eight.

Lefty/Left-hander

Meaning: Any Player whose naturally-dominant *throwing arm* is his left, regardless as to on which side he bats. *See,* Southpaw

The local, "Lefty-Gomez," batted right but was a Southpaw on the hill.

Lights Out/On Fire

Meaning: Playing at an uncharacteristically high level of skill.

Second-baseman, Terry Thomas, has been lights out tonight with three spectacular defensive plays, on top of a double, a triple and five runs batted in.

Line Drive/Screamer/Rope/Seed

Meaning: A solidly hit, batted ball with a low trajectory.

Veteran Third-baseman stepping into the box, here's the pitch, and he slams a screamer *to left field for a base hit.*

Line Drive in the Scorebook

Meaning: A base hit resulting from a nubber or blooper but in the scorebook, as a 1B base hit, it looks the same as a line drive base hit.

Off the tip of the bat, it's a dribbler towards short, Terrence Smith beats out the throw and it'll be a line drive in the scorebook.

Lineup

Meaning: The official, written sequence of Batters from the first to the ninth Player in the batting order, and as amended by substitutions during the game.

Quigley is out of the lineup with a day off, and rookie Bill Montgomery bats fifth for the New Orleans Tide.

Lineup Card

Meaning: A rectangular card on which the lineup of each team is written, and with spaces for substitutions during the game.

Managers for the Baltimore Suns and El Paso Herd just exchanged lineup cards and this Division playoff game is about to get underway!

Lit Up

Meaning: When a Pitcher who had been pitching effectively, allows a Batter to hit the ball very hard for a base hit or extra bases.

Raddison had his no-hitter going for five and a third innings but he just got lit up by Humberto Gonzales with a line shot to right center.

Live Arm

Meaning: A Player, and most typically a Pitcher, who has a very strong throwing arm.

The one thing I like about Pitcher Skip Johnson over there at Wilson High School is that he's got a live arm and things happen when he lets loose.

Load the Bases/Bases Full/ Bases Loaded

Meaning: Where, through a combination of at-bats, a team has baserunners on first, second and third base.

With a one run lead, two outs in the bottom of the ninth, and two runners in scoring position, the Pelicans smartly elected to give Bradley Thompson a free pass to load the bases.

Lock Up (a Player)

Meaning: To tie a Player down to a particular baseball team by a contract covering multiple years.

You know, we locked up that high school senior, Jim Braddock, for…I can tell you this much…less than a hundred Gs signing bonus.

Long Ball

Meaning: A strategy of a team to win the game primarily through hitting Home Runs or hits deep to the outfield for extra base hits.

The Eagles have been playing long ball all afternoon, and it's worked out well so far with a score of Eagles 11, Titans 2.

Long Out

Meaning: A ball hit deeply to the outfield in fair territory, which is caught for an out.

Yastremski hammered that ball to deep center, but with Upjohn tracking it down, it just became a long out.

Long Reliever/Middle Reliever

Meaning: A Relief Pitcher who will pitch for more than a single inning, typically entering the game before the 5th inning where the Starter is struggling, injured or for any other reason cannot continue.

Sengi retired early and the Seals will bring in Long Reliever, Willie Marchini.

Long Strike

Meaning: A deeply hit ball into foul territory.

If it's fair, it's a home run and it is...foul, just a long strike.

Look the Runner Back/Look (a baserunner) Back

Meaning: Where the Pitcher glances over at a baserunner who had taken a lead, so as to keep that runner close to the bag and make it more difficult for the runner to steal the next base.

That is three times now that Targa has looked Brooks back to first base.

Lose a Hitter

Meaning: To walk a hitter, especially if the Pitcher was previously ahead on the count or had a full count on the hitter.

Garfield had Uchimata on the ropes, but through a ten-pitch at-bat, he finally lost him, loading the bases.

Lost the Ball

Meaning: When a fielder loses sight of the ball because of the sun or overcast conditions.

It's a routine fly ball, a can o' corn but wait—Willis can't see the ball, he's lost the ball and it drops...FAIR!

Loud Out

Meaning: When the crowd cheers at what they think is a deeply hit home run, but only to discover that the ball is caught by an outfielder.

It was hit far and deep, and the crowd was all over it, but in the end, it was just a loud out.

Louisiana Ball

Meaning: A ball pitched so fast that it soars right bayou (pun for: by you).

Whoa, and Carlson's head is spinning from that Louisiana Ball!

Low

Meaning: Any pitched ball that crosses the vicinity of the plate beneath the strike zone.

Called strike three and Rivera's out on a pitch that was clearly and absolutely low.

Low and Away/Low and Outside

Meaning: Any pitched ball that crosses the vicinity of the plate both beneath and outside of the strike zone.

Reynosa's 93rd pitch is low and away for ball four, to load the bases and there will be a Pitcher change.

Lumber

Meaning: The club-like instrument which hitters use to bat the ball in baseball.

Mighty Joe Stevens steps out of the dugout with his personalized 36-inch lumber and fully intends to use this lethal weapon for good measure.

M

Major League Baseball/MLB/The Show/Big League/The Bigs

Meaning: The highest level of professional baseball on the North American continent.

After four long years bouncing around the Minors, Olsen finally got his shot in the Bigs, and he took full advantage with a lead-off home run.

Make a Play

Meaning: To attempt to catch, throw or receive a ball in order to make an out or otherwise stop a runner from advancing or scoring.

Eisenstadt scooped that ball up and threw it, off-balance on the run, to make the play.

Make Him Pitch Strikes

Meaning: Common and very good advice to Batters to not chase balls and to wait for actual strikes to go after.

From the stands, his dad yelled out, "Make him pitch strikes, Jackie!", and Jackie did just that, yiketty yak!

Make (the Pitcher) Work

Meaning: For a hitter to lay off of balls and foul off strikes to stay alive and make the Pitcher throw more and more pitches.

Madison's at-bat resulted in a ground-out but did he make Houston work using up eleven pitches!

Make-up Call

Meaning: An incorrect call of Ball or Strike intended by the Umpire to make up for a previous incorrect (or, "bad") call which the Umpire recognizes was mistaken.

That was clearly a make-up call on a pitch catching the inside corner, and the count is now three and two.

Make-up Game

Meaning: A baseball game added to the previously existing schedule and designed to make-up for a game which didn't take place for some reason, such as being rained out.

Well, folks, as a result of this rainout, the Sparrows and Hawks will have a make-up game sometime in the month of August.

Manager/Skip

Meaning: As distinguished from Coaches, a Manager in baseball is the head coach who decides on the lineup, decides when to make substitutions in the lineup, often decides what pitches the Catcher is to signal to the Pitcher, often decides whether a baserunner is to attempt a steal, and who supervises the other coaches such as the Third-base Coach, the First base Coach, the Pitching Coach and the Batting Coach.

Skip, I don't know what it is, but I'm feeling amazing right now—I mean, I'm gonna kill it out there if you can fit me into this game.

Manufacturing Runs

Meaning: Using adept skills and strategy to produce a series of runs for one's team.

And yet another run, piling up runs, manufacturing runs— this time with a squeeze bunt.

Meat (of the bat)

Meaning: The sweet spot of the bat, near the end, although not the very end of the business end of the bat; the area where Batters want to contact the pitched ball.

Swanson hit it hard, but not with the meat of the bat and it's a can o' corn for Center-fielder, Jock Severson.

Meat/Heart (of the lineup)

Meaning: The series of strongest Batters in a team's lineup; typically in the middle of the batting order.

The Pinnipeds have the meat of the lineup coming up in the top of the ninth.

Meatball/Cookie/Fat Pitch

Meaning: A pitch that is in the strike zone and relatively easy to hit.

Now fans, that was a fat pitch and Simpson sends this one way gone!

Mendoza Line

Meaning: The Mendoza Line, named after a Player named Mario Mendoza, means a batting average of .200.

The rookie had a tough month, but finally reached the Mendoza Line after nineteen regular season games.

Middle Infielders

Meaning: The Second-baseman and the Shortstop.

Middle Infielders Teo Mandalay at Short, and Skip Stevens at Second, were magicians at turning a double-play.

Middle of an Inning

Meaning: After the top of the inning and before the bottom of the inning commences.

It's the middle of the fifth inning and I believe the Panthers will be sending in their long-Reliever Henry Higginbotham to pitch.

Minor Leagues/Minors

Meaning: The development leagues for professional baseball.

Zander Edwards kicked around the Minors for three seasons, and at 21 years of age, is coming up to the Majors for a cup of coffee.

Mister (October/Clutch/May/RBI/Everything)

Meaning: Indicating a Player who is exceptionally strong at a particular time or in a particular key situation (*e.g.*, RBIs with a Player in scoring position).

On the Barnstormers, Price rightfully has the handle of "Mister October" for his post-season run-production.

Money Pitch

Meaning: A Pitcher's best pitch, sometimes reserved for a critical moment or the final pitch of a strike-out.

Seven's stock-in-trade is the four-seamer, but his money pitch *is the cutter.*

Moon Shot

Meaning: A home run that is particularly deep and high.

On DigiTake, that moon shot by Pearce was 487 feet!

Morning Journal

Meaning: A bat constructed from poor-quality lumber.

Fogerty needs to get rid of that morning journal, and pick up a new bat supplier.

Most Valuable Player/MVP

Meaning: A Player in a particular league, or a particular post-season series, voted by a designated body as the best overall baseball Player contributing the most for his team.

Right-fielder, Jerry Scanlan, was voted MVP of the Division Series earning that honor with no errors, 16 RBIs, 5 runs, a batting average of .400 and a slugging percentage of .724.

Mound/Pitcher's Mound/Hill/Bump

Meaning: The raised, composite area inside the diamond from which a Pitcher sets up for the pitch and *pitches the ball to a Batter.*

Clancy took the hill tonight, knowing that this was likely to be the very last time he would pitch as a professional baseball Player.

Mound Visit/Pow Wow

Meaning: When the Manager, Pitching Coach, Catcher or Middle Infielder makes a trip to the pitching mound to speak to the Pitcher or for purposes of strategic delay.

Manager Yelson of the Phoenix Rams shook his head and walked out to the mound for a bit of a pow wow with struggling Ace, Sebastian Harding.

Movement (of a pitched ball)

Meaning: The propensity of a pitched ball to move in one direction or another.

Peterson wasn't much for a curve or changeup, but there's no doubt whatsoever that he got plenty of movement on his speed pitches.

Muff It (the ball)

Meaning: To fail to cleanly field a hit ball.

That ground ball should have been a piece of cake, but instead, Phil Novello shamefully muffed it.

Muscle

Meaning: A baseball Player.

The Dallas Sanddabs paid fifty-thousand on the muscle to lock up high school senior, Jeremy Gwinn.

Mustard

Meaning: An element of high speed in a throw or a pitched ball.

The beleaguered Manager shouted to Shortstop, Willy Sturdevant, to "put some mustard" on his throws from now on.

Nasty Curve

Meaning: A particularly effective breaking ball pitch.

Peterson backed away from that nasty curveball.

Neighborhood Play

Meaning: The unwritten rule that allows a middle infielder to slide his foot simply in the general vicinity of the second base bag (without actually having to touch the base) when turning a force-out double play.

Burrows to Taylor to Pierson in a neighborhood play for outs two and three to end the inning.

No Decision

Meaning: How a Starting Pitcher's outing is officially recorded when he neither qualifies as the winning, nor as the losing, Pitcher in a game.

After his rehab stint in the Minors, Starter Bradley was happy, in his first outing at the Show, to get a No Decision.

No-hitter

Meaning: Where the pitching staff of a team allows no Batter to reach base safely off of a base hit of any variety.

The Colts' Bullpen had a no-hitter going into the bottom of the ninth inning, spoiled only by a game-winning home run by the Ravens' Shortstop, Lance Reynolds.

No Pitch

Meaning: When time is called prior to a pitch being thrown, or for any other reason, play is halted during a Pitcher's pitch.

When a 96 mile an hour fastball hit a humming bird mid-flight, it was called a "no pitch" by the Blue.

Nowhere to Put Him

Meaning: Where the bases are loaded and the Pitcher starts to throw pitches which are called balls, a walk will result in a run scoring.

The Star Fish have the bases loaded, the count on Vallejo is 2 and 2 and there's nowhere to put 'im.

Nubber/Squibber

Meaning: A ball hit off the end or close to the end of a Batter's bat, so as to turn the batted ball into a ball of very low power.

That was a pure nubber, trickling towards Shortstop, and "Legs" Fernandez runs it out for a base hit.

Obstruction

Meaning: When a fielder, not holding the ball and not in the act of fielding it, impedes the progress of a baserunner. *See,* Interference

Shortstop, Bill Evans, inadvertently moved into the path of Garner rounding second, causing a collision and resulting in an obstruction call by Third-base Umpire, Roy Stevens.

O'fer

Meaning: Referring to the fact that a particular Player got no hits for all of his at-bats in a particular game; short for "O" for X number of at-bats.

Not particularly productive in today's game, Hornswoggle went O'fer.

Off-speed Pitch

Meaning: Any pitch that is significantly slower than the Pitcher's fastball.

Their Ace had him in the hole, until Haroldson went yiketty yak with his off-speed pitch.

Off the Hook

Meaning: When, because of his team making a rally on offense, a Pitcher is no longer deemed responsible for the loss of a game.

The Sentinels rack up eight runs in the bottom of the fifth inning and Oppenheimer is officially off the hook for that nightmare top of the fifth debacle.

On Base Percentage/OBP

Meaning: During the on-going season, hits + walks + hit by pitch divided by plate appearances (except not when a sacrifice bunt is involved).

After 20 games in the season, Early's OBP is a respectable .458.

On-deck (noun re: sequence of batters)

Meaning: The next Batter in the lineup after the current at-bat is completed.

Paddington steps into the box, with Bristlebaum on-deck and Rex Rittenthorpe in the hole.

On-deck Circle

Meaning: The literally circled area (in white chalk) where the on-deck Batter is expected to warm-up awaiting his at-bat.

Now in the on-deck circle, Jack Wayne slid the donut onto his bat, warming up.

One-hitter

Meaning: A game in which the Pitcher (or Pitchers) has allowed only one Batter to reach base safely on a batted ball.

Going into the bottom of the 8th inning, Patterson has a very clean one-hitter going, as the Wild Cats lead the Bull Dogs three nothing.

One-hopper

Meaning: A batted ground ball that bounces only once before being fielded by an infielder.

It's a routine one-hopper to Escobar at Short and...oh, he bobbles it...but makes the throw to first for out number two.

On the Board

Meaning: When a team initially scores one or more runs, and the runs are posted on the scoreboard.

They still have work to do but are finally on the board with Teasdale's bomb to the left field grandstands, and the score is now Nomads 1, Sharks 7.

On the Bump

Meaning: Referring to who is pitching at that particular moment.

Taylor was worked over by the Kings, and long-Reliever Randy Peabody is now on the bump in the top of the fourth inning.

On the Hook

Meaning: When a Pitcher, in jeopardy of being responsible for a loss, leaves a game.

With the bases full and two outs in the seventh, in a three-three tie, Perkins is on the hook as he exits stage left.

On the Skids/Skids

Meaning: A lengthy losing streak for either a Pitcher, or a team.

The Lions have been on the skids now for the past 25 games, with a record of 3 and 22, and tonight their Ace, if you can still call him that, will try, again, for his first win of the season.

Open Base

Meaning: Any base not occupied by a baserunner, and especially, when any two bases are occupied but one base is not.

Manager DeNiro elects to give a free pass to Underwood and fill up the open base at first.

Opposite Field

Meaning: For a hitter who bats right, his opposite field is considered to be right field, and *vice versa* for a hitter who bats left.

That was a four-seamer to the outside of the plate and Vernon hammered it to the opposite field for a stand-up double.

Ordinary Effort

Meaning: The standard by which a muffed play will be designated as an error to the defensive Player, such that if the play would have been successful with ordinary effort at that particular level of league play, the mistake will be deemed a fielding error.

Wentworth dove for that ball, got to his feet and air-mailed the ball over first, which is not ordinary effort and will certainly be ruled an error.

Out

Meaning: When a Batter or baserunner is declared to be one of three outs, either by a strike out, a fly out, a force out or a tag out. On a strikeout or close play at any base, an Umpire's signal for a call of out is raising up his right fist and making one quick, hammering motion in a downward direction.

The ruling on the field is "out" at second on the steal attempt, but we'll see if that changes on video-review.

Outfielder

Meaning: A Player whose defensive assignment is either left field, center field or right field.

Sandy Topperman is first and foremost an outfielder, but can also be a middle infielder if needed by the Jets.

Outing

Meaning: Whenever a Pitcher is put into the game to pitch.

Today will mark Quigley's third outing since his elbow surgery, and Manager O'Leary plans to let him go for up to 40 pitches, give or take.

Out of Reach (the game)

Meaning: When the score is so lopsided (for example, 15 to 2 in the 8th inning) that the losing team considers the game to be highly unlikely to win and begins to conserve its resources, such as Relief Pitchers.

At a score of 12-3 in the top of the 9th inning, the Guardians considered the game to be out of reach, and put their back-up Shortstop in to pitch, just wanting the game to end.

Outside

Meaning: Describing when a pitch is out of the strike zone, to the far side, away from the Batter (as opposed to "Inside," to the near side, close to the Batter).

Candelora swings and misses for strike three on a ball well outside; and Yoder has just pitched a perfect game!

P

Painting the Corners/Paint the Strike Zone/
Throwing Paint/Paint the Black

Meaning: To throw pitches which cross the plate on the edges of the rectangular, virtual strike zone.

Snyder's been throwing paint tonight, fanning eight so far and pitching a no-hitter, thus far, to boot.

Passed Ball

Meaning: A determination made by an on-site baseball official, indicating an absence of ordinary skill by the Catcher in catching a pitch, in which case a run scored as a result of the mistake is not counted as an earned run against the Pitcher.

It was a passed ball but no runners advanced.

Patience/Patient Hitter/Plate Discipline

Meaning: Referring to a desirable state of mind in batting, where you refrain from helping out the Pitcher by swinging at balls, and instead wait for pitches which cross the plate inside the strike zone. *See*: Make Him Pitch Strikes

Any hitting coach will tell you that focus, patience and fast hands are a few of the primary keys to hitting a pitched baseball.

Payoff Pitch

Meaning: The first pitch after the count becomes full on the Batter.

It's the payoff pitch and Tinsdale…swings and slaps a Texas Leaguer…for a base hit.

Pea

Meaning: A thrown or batted ball at particularly high speed.

Worthy just hurled a 102 miles an hour pea for strike three to strike out Smith, looking.

Peeking

Meaning: When a Batter glances down to try to pick up a physical pitch sign from the Catcher, or to catch a glimpse at where the Catcher is framing the pitch.

With contemporary radio technology, peeking is rapidly becoming a forgotten art in professional baseball.

Pepper

Meaning: An often-banned practice drill where multiple Players soft-toss a pitch to a Batter, who swings easily to knock slow grounders to one of the Players, who in turn soft-tosses another pitch to the Batter.

The ground crew Chief blew his top when he noticed five visiting team Players playing pepper and tearing up the infield grass in the process.

The Pennant

Meaning: A team achieves this award-status upon winning a league championship.

It's a beautiful day at the ballpark for the fifth and deciding game between the Oklahoma City Troubadours and the Kansas City Roughriders for the Pennant.

Perfect Game

Meaning: A game in which the winning team does not allow a single Batter of the losing team to reach any base safely by any means.

The Southpaw, Billy Wells, just hurled a nine-inning perfect game, as the Phoenix Tumbleweeds blanked the Eli Prairie Dogs, seven zero.

Picked Off

Meaning: When a baserunner leads off from the base and is tagged out by a defensive Player off a throw from the Pitcher.

Gerogio had a walking lead at first, and with a snap throw from the Southpaw, Vestermark, Georgio was picked off.

Pick-off Move/Pick-off

Meaning: A Pitcher's deceptive throw to one of the bases to catch a runner off of the base.

Holden has an excellent pick-off move, which Euker is about to find out if he…and he just did!

Pick It Clean

Meaning: When an infielder adeptly fields a hard-hit ground ball.

Hard grounder to Short and Sonny Peckinpah picks it clean and makes the throw for out number one in the top of the fourth.

Pickle/Rundown

Meaning: Where a baserunner is trapped by fielders in a base path as the fielders work together to try to tag him out.

Martingale is caught in a rundown now, but he's quick on his feet and he...slips under the tag, back to second base safely.

Pinch Hit

Meaning: To substitute in for another Player who would otherwise have been next to bat.

Sanders to pinch hit for Paulson, who continues to be in a slump.

Pinch Hitter

Meaning: The Player who substitutes in for another Player who is about to bat.

The Rockets will almost certainly pinch hit for Elway, and the pinch hitter will be...Steve Simmons.

Pinch Runner

Meaning: The Player who substitutes in for another Player who is already on base, typically in order to have a faster and more adept baserunner on base.

> *And, no surprise at this critical point in the game, Hoyt Hogan will sub in as pinch runner for Manning.*

Pine Tar

Meaning: A foreign substance allowed for use by players on up to 18 inches of a bat handle, to improve the Batter's grip.

> *In the hole, Rowdy Wilson has the pine tar rag and is getting that extra grip on his maple bat handle as permitted by league rules.*

Pitch/Offering (noun)

Meaning: A Pitcher throwing a baseball to the Catcher when the Batter is in the Batter's box during his at-bat.

> *Mooney's offering to Elway is a slider, in there for strike one.*

Pitch/Offer (verb)

Meaning: The act of a Pitcher throwing a pitch to his Catcher.

> *Baserunners at the corners, Pillsbury into the stretch, and pitches a four-seamer, outside for Ball 2; 2 and "O" on the count.*

Pitch Around

Meaning: To pitch anything that the Batter cannot hit, in a strategic decision similar to offering the Batter a free pass.

Olemar is such a dangerous hitter that Courtier chooses to pitch around him.

Pitch Clock/Pitch Timer

Meaning: A timing system established to speed up the game and to lower the average total times for completed games, where Pitchers have only a set number of seconds to pitch the ball, and Batters have a time limit by which they must be ready in the Batter's box, as exhibited in a digital clock for the Players, Umpires and spectators.

The pitch clock was initially viewed by Pitchers and Batters as a nuisance, but presently is accepted as an integral part of pro ball.

Pitch Count

Meaning: The ongoing number of pitches thrown by a particular Pitcher against Batters in the game.

Severson is hanging on by a thread and his pitch count, in the top half of the fifth inning, is 107.

Pitcher/Hurler/Ace/Arm

Meaning: The Player who is on the mound and throwing the ball toward the plate to somehow get the Batter out.

Kendal Jackson will step in as Pitcher for the Minneapolis Seals.

Pitcher-friendly Strike

Meaning: A ball crossing just outside of the strike zone but called a strike by the Plate Umpire.

Low and inside, a Pitcher-friendly strike to Ortiz.

Pitching

Meaning: When a Pitcher is on the mound to pitch, or from the mound pitches, toward the Catcher, behind home plate, in an effort to get one or more outs.

Pitching for the Gators in today's game is Jack Forbes, whose record on the season is four and one.

Pitch-out (rare in contemporary baseball)

Meaning: A pitch deliberately thrown out of reach of a Batter, designed to enable the Catcher to more easily throw out a baserunner attempting to steal a base.

Painter has quite a lead and with two outs…there he goes and it's a pitch-out and Catcher Sam Flowers rockets the throw to second for the tag out.

Plate Appearance

Meaning: Each and every completed turn batting, regardless of the outcome.

Taylor was greeted by high-fives all around following his successful plate appearance with a sac-fly and yet another RBI to his credit.

Platoon/Platooning

Meaning: When two or more Players trade off playing at a particular fielding position.

The Skip has Greninger, batting left, and Marsden, batting right, platooning in center field.

Play

Meaning: Any action or maneuver by one or more Players in advancing the offensive or defensive goals of their team in a baseball game.

With runners at the corners and one out in the seventh, the hit-and-run play was on with Billings up to bat.

Play Ball

Meaning: A phrase which may be called out by the Home Plate Umpire to start the baseball game.

Around ten minutes following the National Anthem, the Home Plate Umpire bellowed out, "Play Ball!" and the first pitch was soon thrown.

Pop Fly/Pop-up

Meaning: Any batted ball, in fair or foul territory, infield or short outfield, which is hit mostly in a vertical direction.

It's a routine pop fly for Remmington, who makes a clean catch for the second out of the inning.

Position Player

Meaning: Any baseball Player, other than Pitcher, who on defense is an infielder, an outfielder or a Catcher.

Early was a position Player in the Minors, but the Indiana Turtles have him as a Designated Hitter.

Pro Ball

Meaning: Any professional baseball league (*i.e.*, where the Players are paid to play baseball), including regional independent leagues, the Minor Leagues and the Major League.

Winston's life-long dream was to play pro ball, and now he's finally made it, with the Cottonwood, Arizona, Devil Dusters.

Protect the Runner

Meaning: In a case where a coach signals for a base steal (and where it is not a hit and run situation), the Batter will either swing or not swing at the upcoming pitch, with one factor being the Batter's assessment of which will help the runner be successful in his steal attempt.

With the "steal" sign on, and knowing that Thomas was on the slow-side of Major League baserunners, Wilson was determined to swing at the pitch regardless of whether it was over the plate.

Push-Bunt

Meaning: To firmly bunt a ball past a charging infielder or Pitcher.

Hopkins arrives safely at first, thanks to his flawless push-bunt.

Put Out

Meaning: To tag a baserunner for an out, with the ball or with the Player's glove containing the ball, at any time when the baserunner is in jeopardy. *Distinguish,* Force Out

Jenkins tried to stretch his single to left into a double, but was put out by Singleton after an outstanding throw by Left-fielder, Bob Ellis.

Putting on a Clinic

Meaning: Whenever a Player performs his role in a particularly exceptional manner.

Clancy has been putting on a clinic at third base today, with that diving catch as one example of his quality play.

Quality At-bat

Meaning: An at-bat where the Batter swung primarily at pitches in the strike zone, used up a lot of pitches by the Pitcher, thereby significantly pushing up the pitch count, and accomplished some important goal on offense such as attaining an RBI.

Babbit had a quality at-bat, over the course of 18 pitches, knocking in a run and reaching base safely.

Quick-pitch

Meaning: When a Pitcher makes his pitch without the usual delivery protocols, in an effort to catch a Batter unprepared to deal with the pitch.

Although perfectly legal, Bernstein's proclivity to quick-pitch makes him a very unpopular Pitcher with opposing teams.

Quiet Bats

Meaning: When a team is, for any reason, not making good contact with the ball in its various at-bats.

The Star Links had very quiet bats tonight, as evidenced by the shut out of 7-zero.

R

Railroad

Meaning: Where a baserunner deliberately barrels into a position Player in order to attempt to dislodge the ball, or to gain access to the plate or bag blocked by a defensive Player.

Victor Hozenozelle was notorious for his penchant for railroading middle infielders to break up double plays, and many a bruhaha has erupted over his actions.

Rain Delay

Meaning: When a game is delayed in its starting time, or play is temporarily suspended due to rain or other severely inclement weather, such as snow or lightning.

There's a rain delay of the game; but we'll wait and see if the game resumes, okay?

Rained Out/Rainout

Meaning: When a game cannot start or finish due to rain or other severely inclement weather, such as snow or lightning.

I checked online and the game's canceled for a rainout, but we'll go another time.

Rally Cap

Meaning: Wearing one's hat inside-out or backwards as a playful superstition in hopes of one's team coming back in late innings from a run deficit to win the game.

Every single person in our row had their rally caps on and we all knew the Sentinels could win!

Rang 'im Up (verb)

Meaning: When a Pitcher strikes out a Batter. *See*, Strikes Out

And Forester rang 'im up with a splitter, for the win.

Read (a pitch)

Meaning: A Batter's effort to rapidly see and understand what pitch is heading his way, so as to help him decide whether to swing and if so, how to make good contact with the ball.

Prescott wasn't much of a long-ball hitter, but he consistently had a good read on the ball, and his on-base percentage was through the roof.

Regulation Game

Meaning: A baseball game that ends in the 9th inning, or, if shortened by conditions of play, at least five completed innings.

It's in the books as a regulation game, following a one and one-half hour rain delay.

Relay/Relay Play

Meaning: Where an outfielder throws the ball to in infielder, to be thrown to another Player, or held, by the infielder in his discretion. *See*, Cut-off Man

From deep center field, Willis threw a relay to Abbott, who threw to Geffner at the plate for the tag out.

Release On Waivers

Meaning: When a ball club releases rights to a Player subject to the claiming ball club assuming responsibility for fulfilling any remaining obligations pursuant to the Player contract.

Rebels fans were, of course, disappointed when Petey Peterson was released on waivers, but they were happy to see the Triple-A, Catcher-phenom, Burt Kilpatrick, brought up after four years in the Minors.

Relief Pitcher/Reliever

Meaning: A Pitcher who is brought into a game to pitch after the starting Pitcher, or another Relief Pitcher, is removed from the game due to a high pitch count, fatigue, poor performance or some other strategic reason.

Reliever Ronald Rowlings enters the game with an impressive one-point-O O ERA.

Retire (a Batter)

Meaning: For a Pitcher to secure an out from a Batter by a strikeout, ground-out or fly-out.

Ireland retired Vitaly on two pitches, and now, slugger Bob Houseman steps into the box.

Retire the Side

Meaning: For a Pitcher to secure three outs in an inning, regardless of the method and regardless of hits or runs in the inning.

Massani retired the side with only one hit and no runs in the bottom of the fourth.

Retire the Side in Order/Side Retired in Order/Three Up, Three Down

Meaning: For a Pitcher to secure three outs in an inning, regardless of the method, but with none of the first three Batters safely reaching a base.

Arturo Perez retires the side in order and the score stands, Pelicans 3, Sparrows 4.

Rhubarb

Meaning: A serious, prolonged and widespread argument or fight during a game.

The Mavericks were warned, Stevens hit Jones in the back with a 95 miles an hour fastball, and the rhubarb is in full swing.

Rifle

Meaning: A very hard and accurate throw in a defensive play.

A ground ball, and Singleton scoops it and effortlessly rifles it across the diamond for the final out of the inning.

Right-center Gap

Meaning: The part of the outfield between right field and center field where a well-hit ball will likely lead to extra bases.

Parson's fly ball deep to the right-center gap will take him to a stand-up double.

Right Field/Right

Meaning: The fair-territory part of the playing field comprising the outfield grass generally to the Catcher's right of the baseball diamond.

It's a line shot to right, and Peterson's throw will hold Moravek to a single.

Right-fielder

Meaning: The Player who, on defense, is an outfielder in right field.

Right-fielder, Jerry Scanlan, has a veritable canon for an arm.

Right in (a Batter's) Kitchen

Meaning: A pitched ball that crosses the plate in the hitter's power zone.

That ball is long gone and was right in Yastrzemski's kitchen.

Righty/Right-hander

Meaning: Any Player whose naturally-dominant *throwing arm* is his right, regardless as to on which side he bats.

Center-fielder Josh Pendergrass batted left but was a right-hander in the field.

Rip

Meaning: For a Batter to hit a pitched ball with exceptional force and velocity.

Okajima absolutely ripped that ball and it is way long gone for his 32nd four-bagger of the season.

Road Trip

Meaning: When a team leaves its home field for a sequence of games with opposing teams at their respective home fields.

And with that win, the Huskies launch tonight on an out-of-this-world, twelve-day road trip, to play the Stars, Galaxies and Comets.

Robbed

Meaning: The way a Batter might feel when a fielder makes a play so spectacular that it turns a hit or homerun into an out.

That ball is high and it's deep and it is…caught in an amazing leap by Flint at the center field fence, and oh was Casper robbed of a dinger.

Room Service

Meaning: A ball hit so directly to a fielder that he barely needs to move in order to catch it.

Clancy's served up room service on that one-hopper, and he makes a clean pick and perfect throw to first for the out.

Rope/Frozen Rope/Line Drive/Canon Shot

Meaning: A ball hit so hard and with such a flat trajectory, that it appears to lose no height for most of its flight off the bat.

Oh, what an absolute canon shot, a frozen rope, off the bat of William Arthur for a well-needed single!

Rosin Bag

Meaning: As suggested, it is a small cloth bag filled with a rosin powder that when used in moderation and without addition of any other substance, is not prohibited in baseball and may improve a Pitcher's grip on the ball for pitching.

Humphreys picks up the rosin bag, drops the bag, shakes the excess off his pitching hand, steps up to the pitcher's rubber, grips the ball...and is set.

Rotation/Starting Rotation (of Pitchers)

Meaning: A team's recurring sequence of starting Pitchers, which affords each a period of about five to six days between starts.

The Mustangs rotation will be broken for tonight's game, with Bjerke jumping forward to pitch against the Tigers on only three days' rest.

Rubber/Pitcher's Plate

Meaning: A white-rubber strip on the Pitcher's Mound from which the Pitcher pushes off in his pitching to a Batter.

Petrovski's in contact with the rubber, hears the sign, moves into his set position… steps away, firing the ball to pick-off of Morris at first!

Run(s)

Meaning: The scoring computational element in a game of baseball, where at the end of the game, the team with the most of these wins. A run is awarded to the team whose baserunner advances all the way around the bases of the diamond safely.

Peterson allowed three runs in six innings on five hits, and with five strikeouts.

Run on Contact

Meaning: With two outs, *not* a full count, and baserunners in a force situation (they must progress to the next base on a fair ball), the baserunners will run immediately when the Batter hits the ball, since they are forced to progress, or a walk or hit by pitch will advance the forced runners, or a strikeout, ground out or fly out will otherwise end the half inning. *Distinguish*, Send the Runners

Bases full, two outs, count of two and one, they all know, it's run on contact.

Runners at the Corners/Runners on the Corners

Meaning: When baserunners are on first base and third base.

*With runners at the corners and one out, Tim Dorsey subs in
to pinch run at first for Catcher, Ronny Reynolds.*

Run Batted In/RBI/Ribbie/Ribeye/Steak/Runs Knocked In

Meaning: A Batter's statistic which counts the number of runs
scored as a result of his run-scoring batted balls (except if a ground
ball to a double play), and bases-loaded walks or hit by pitch.

*Hartley is racking up the RBIs today, with eight, off of two
home runs, a double and two singles.*

Rundown (noun)

Meaning: When a baserunner is off of a base, between Players
on the defense who are attempting to tag him out. *See,* Pickle

*Taglio has himself in a rundown between third and home—he's
scrambling and…ducks under the tag and safely back to third.*

S

Sabermetrics

Meaning: A system of acquiring data and creating baseball statistics useful in evaluating Player performance.

According to Sabermetrics, outfielder Dale Martin is sorely undervalued in the current market.

Sacrifice Bunt/Sac Bunt/SAC

Meaning: A bunt play, before there are two outs, where the primary goal is to advance a runner to the next base, and the secondary goal is for the Batter to reach first base safely. *Distinguish,* Squeeze Play and Suicide Squeeze

Runners at first and second and Venne pivots to a sac bunt, lays it down and both runners go station to station, while Venne is thrown out at first.

Sacrifice Fly/Sac Fly/SF

Meaning: With fewer than two outs, a hit to the outfield on the fly, which is caught for an out, but which successfully enables a baserunner to score. A Sac Fly does not count as an at-bat for the Batter, and thus, does not factor in to a Player's batting average.

Granger Timsley was hoping to go yard, but was satisfied with his game-tying sac fly to deep center field.

Safe

Meaning: When a baserunner reaches a base or home plate and, pursuant to the rules of baseball, he is entitled to the base. On a close play, an Umpire's signal for a call of safe is extending his arms out to the sides, palms down.

It's a bang-bang play, with the call on the field of safe, but this one's going to video review.

Save

Meaning: When a Relief Pitcher enters a game to preserve his team's lead, he maintains the lead through the end of the game and any one of the following occurs: at his entry, his team has a lead of no more than three runs and he pitches at least one full inning (*i.e.*, three outs); at his entry, the tying run is on-deck, on base or batting; or, he pitches no fewer than three innings, no matter the score.

It was good morning, good afternoon and good night for Billingsly in the top of the ninth for his fourth save of the season.

Save Situation

Meaning: When a pitcher enters a game to pitch and his successful performance could lead to a save.

Perkins was no stranger to a save situation, and he entered the game having every intention to shut down the Sharks' offense.

Saw-off

Meaning: When a pitched ball contacts a hitter's bat near the handle in the course of a swing, and the ball breaks the bat into two or more sections.

The sawed-off barrel of Peterman's bat just exploded across the mound.

Score (noun)

Meaning: The running tally of runs accumulated by each baseball team against the other.

With three runs across in the fourth, the score stands at Orlando 7, Pittsburg 11.

Score/Scoring (verb)

Meaning: The act of a baserunner touching home plate under circumstances where it counts as a run.

Yardly scores and continues the blow-out of, now, 14 – nothing, over the Miami Palms.

Scoring Position

Meaning: A baserunner or baserunners on second base, third base, or second and third bases.

The Penguins trying to cash in on their runners in scoring position, but once again, that bird can't fly!

Scout/Baseball Man

Meaning: A professional at searching for promising prospects to sign for a professional baseball club.

The Players on both teams were well aware that the middle-aged, black male sitting seven rows back behind home plate was a scout; but for what club, they did not know.

Screwball/Fader/Scroogie

Meaning: *A pitch which fades to the same side from which it was thrown.*

Tinsdale struck out Roiles, with a mind-bending screwball.

Season

Meaning: The period of time after Spring Training until the finish of league play, prior to the post-season playoffs and Championship.

It's only the second week of the season and the Minneapolis Marauders already have two starting Pitchers on the IL.

Second Base/Second

Meaning: The bag directly in line with the Catcher and Pitcher, 90 feet from each of first and third bases, second in a sequence of four, counting home plate.

Bleeker rounds second at a full run, slides head first into third and is...tagged out.

Second-baseman

Meaning: The Player assigned, on defense, to the infield position on the first base side of second base.

Second-baseman Bobbie Rich earned two Platinum Bats in his electric career of fourteen seasons with three Major League teams.

Seeing Eye Single

Meaning: A routine ground ball which manages to slip between two infielders who were unable to make a play on the ball.

Varnish picks up a seeing eye single to advance the runners station-to-station and fill up the bases.

See It!

Meaning: An encouraging tip to a Batter to focus on the pitch and know what it is, where it's headed and when it will get there, in order for the Batter to be able to hit that pitch.

My dad used to always remind me, when I was in the cage during batting practice as a youngster, to "see it!".

Send/Send the Runner

Meaning: In a situation where there are two outs, a full count on the Batter and baserunners are in a force situation, a Coach will signal the force runners to run immediately upon the Pitcher committing to pitch to the Batter. *Distinguish*, Run on Contact

Third Base Coach, Rex Roth, signaled to send the runner on first, giving Bartholemew a great jump.

Sent Down

Meaning: When a Player is removed from the active, Major League, roster of a team and returned to an affiliated team in the Minors.

Willie McPeters was brought up for a cup of coffee by the Regals, but sent down after the All-Star break.

Sent to the Showers

Meaning: Describing a Player who has been ejected from the game, against his will, for any reason.

Following his high and tight brush-back pitch, Storm Thompson was sent to the showers by the Blue.

Series

Meaning: Any set of multiple games in succession between two teams.

The result is that the Freighters and their cross-town rival, the Lions, split the series, two wins each.

Serve Up/Serve

Meaning: To pitch a ball that is routine for a professional hitter to hit hard.

Peabody served up a hanging curve to Riordan, who walloped it out of the park for a home run.

Set Position

Meaning: The act of a Pitcher arriving at one of three stance and arm positionings, after which he must commit to pitch to the Batter or throw to a base in an effort to catch a runner off the base.

Harley in the set position, steps off the rubber and fires to first in a pick-off attempt.

Set the Table/The Table is Set

Meaning: When a Batter gets on base and the next Batter potentially can drive him home.

The Storm Chasers have set the table in four innings but their only run came from a solo home run in the second.

Seventh-inning Stretch

Meaning: A tradition in baseball for a pause between the top half of the seventh inning and the bottom half of the seventh inning, during which the stadium announcer announces that music for, "Take Me Out to the Ballgame" will be played, so that the fans can all stand up, stretch and sing along as the music is played and the lyrics are displayed on the scoreboard.

The fun part of the seventh-inning stretch is that it doesn't matter whether you're a singer, if you just love baseball and enjoy singing along with the crowd.

Shag/Shagging Fly Balls

Meaning: A pregame warmup for the outfielders (or simply outfield practice among friends), where fly balls are hit, typically using a fungo bat, and the fielder who catches the ball throws it back.

Growing up, I used to shag balls, hit by my dad, as a regular part of our practice routine.

Shake Off the Sign

Meaning: When a Pitcher doesn't like the pitch choice given to him and he uses some motion, typically by slightly shaking his head, to indicate he wants to pitch a different pitch.

Youngblood shook off two signs and then got what he wanted—the signal for a splitter.

The Shift

Meaning: A now-outlawed practice of shifting a middle-infielder to the opposite side of second base than normally played for his position, in order to increase the defense on the side of the diamond to which the particular hitter most often hits.

Defense against Denton was very straightforward and effective—employ the shift to the left side of the diamond.

Shine-ball

Meaning: An illegal pitch employing a means to make one part of a baseball slick, to accentuate an erratic movement of a pitch.

Hunter Mayfield surreptitiously used a dab of Vaseline from just behind his right earlobe to perfect his shine-ball curve.

Shoestring Catch

Meaning: When a fielder catches a fly ball, with the back of his glove at or very near the ground at the moment of the catch.

Shortstop, Julio Garcia, makes a diving, shoestring catch, and rolls forward and up, throwing a laser shot to second base for the double-up—what a play!

Short Ball/Small Ball

Meaning: A strategy to win games primarily by manufacturing runs based on base hits, base stealing, sacrifice flies and bunting.

The Ridgeway Commuters didn't have a lot of power hitters, but they were skilled technicians at playing small ball to beat their opponents.

Short-hop

Meaning: When a Player catches a ground ball not at the top of its bounce-arc, but instead, as the ball is still rising from hitting the ground.

McMaster's jump is one of the quickest in the league and he short-hopped that grounder to make the play against the speedy lefty, Ronald Bean.

Shortstop/Short

Meaning: The Player assigned, on defense, to the infield position on the third base side of second base.

Shortstop, Tommy Pines, is a scrappy Player, five-foot-nine and about a buck-sixty, who has great jump and range, and good hands.

Show Bunt

Meaning: When a Player feigns a bunt stance and bat position, but then pulls back to either take the pitch or swing away.

Victor's instructions were clear: show bunt and then hit a line drive through the infield to score runners from second and third.

Shutout (noun)

Meaning: Where the winning team holds the loosing team to no runs in the game.

Tonight, the Red Wings got their fifth shutout of the season, equaling their all-time record.

Shut out (verb)

Meaning: A Pitcher or succession of Pitchers for a team holding the opposing team to no runs in the entire game.

Huntington pitched a full nine innings and shut out the Tornados, five zero.

Side-armer

Meaning: A Pitcher who throws the ball in the unorthodox manner of leaning over and having his pitching arm sweep almost parallel to the ground before releasing the ball.

It took the Patrons one rotation through the lineup to figure out how to destroy the side-armer, Klaus Fleischmann.

Sign (a Player)

Meaning: To tie up a Player contractually to play baseball for a certain team, whether in the Minors or in the Majors.

In the old days, you could sign a Player for next to nothing and he's just happy to get off the farm; but these days, it's not uncommon to give a million bucks-plus to sign a top prospect right out of high school.

Sign(s)

Meaning: Signals of any kind from any Player, Manager or Coach to a Player or Coach as to what play, or pitch, is wanted at a particular point in a baseball game.

Williams picked up the steal sign from the Third Base Coach, got a great jump on the pitch, and dove in safely to second base.

Single

Meaning: From a batted ball, not the result of a fielding error or fielder's choice, in which the Batter safely reaches first base.

Steve Masters leads off for the Palm Desert Eagles with a clean single up the middle.

Sinker/Dropper

Meaning: A fastball with a downward trajectory, generally thrown in a three-quarter arm movement, with the index finger on a vertical seam and the middle finger near the adjacent vertical seam (the "tracks"), rotating inward slightly as the ball is released along the middle finger.

In a full windup, Julio Hernandez unleashed a sinker that froze Beecher for the strikeout.

Sit Him Down/Sets Him Down

Meaning: To strike out a Batter, particularly for a crucial out in the game.

Sets him down *for the Metros to clinch the Pennant!*

Sitting on a Pitch

Meaning: Having an intention of only swinging on a particular pitch that you surmise is coming—for example, a Curve Ball—and thus giving the hitter an advantage (assuming that that pitch is thrown) of "knowing" in advance what pitch is coming.

With a 2 and "O" count, he's probably sitting on a pitch, and if I know Jose, he's sitting on a high fastball.

Sky

Meaning: To hit a towering fly ball.

Naughten literally skied that ball and it is…gone!

Slap Hitter

Meaning: A Batter with marginal power, who strikes out rarely and has a skill for getting hits to anywhere on the diamond. *See,* Spray Hitter

> *Little Joe Parsons was fast, had a good eye for balls and strikes and was an accomplished slap hitter.*

Slice/Slice Foul

Meaning: A ball hit towards the opposite field (*e.g.,* right field for a Batter that bats right) that starts out in fair territory and curves off into foul territory.

> *Rogers seems to hit a lot of slice fouls but it's all good since he drives up the pitch count each at-bat.*

Slide

Meaning: A running baserunner's technique of dropping his body to the ground (usually referring to a feet-first slide, but also including a dive, head-first) once close to the base being approached, in order to reach safely without overrunning the base, and when the intention is to progress only to that base.

> *It's a double-steal, Timberlake fires the ball to third, Jenkins slides in and is…safe.*

Slider

Meaning: Thrown with a sideways rotation, this pitch breaks downward and laterally across the plate. *Distinguish,* Cutter

Mendoza's go-to payoff pitch is a four-seam fastball, but he's also relied on a slider in that situation.

Sliding Mitts

Meaning: Specially crafted, durable, padded mittens, typically worn on the baserunner's left hand or left and right hands, designed to minimize injuries to the hands and fingers when diving into a base he is approaching.

Gary Underhill at first, wearing sliding mitts and always considered a base stealing threat—and there he goes!

Slow Roller

Meaning: A ground ball hit in such a manner that it rolls slowly in the infield, making any play on the Batter very difficult, and to have any chance of a put out, typically requiring a bare hand catch and a throw on the run.

It's a slow roller toward third and Mendoza lets it curve and roll foul where he picks it up for strike two on the Batter.

Slugfest

Meaning: When a team rocks the opposing team's pitching staff, making hit after hit.

Rogues versus Henchmen today was a veritable slugfest—11 nothing, Henchmen.

Slugger

Meaning: A Player who is an effective Batter and commonly gets hits, extra-base hits and home runs.

George Tanner was a slugger, but also a heads-up outfielder.

Slugging Percentage

Meaning: A weighted batting percentage taking into account not only singles, but also doubles, triples and home runs.

For Rumsfeld, his strikeouts were the exception and his high slugging percentage, the rule.

Smoke (a Batter)

Meaning: Hitting a Batter with a pitch.

The fact is, the Stars never liked Paul Mikelson, and their Ace just smoked him.

Snap Throw

Meaning: A quick throw by a Player, with the flick of the wrist, without a full throwing motion.

Catcher Bobby Rich made a snap throw to second to gun down the runner.

Snow Cone

Meaning: Catching a fly ball with the very tips of the glove's fingers and thumb.

Rutherford dives on a full-run and he…makes the catch with a snow cone!

Snowman

Meaning: When a Pitcher is charged with allowing eight runs, or when a team scores eight runs in a single inning.

With that walked-in run, Tanner has a snowman in this contest.

Soft Hands/Good Leather

Meaning: An infielder who is particularly adept at fielding hard-hit ground balls.

Peterman is a force of one when batting, with a .312 batting average; but his soft hands is what sets him apart as a top-tier middle infielder.

Soft Toss

Meaning: A form of batting practice where a coach tosses a ball underhand from one side of a Batter and the Batter swings to hit the ball. Also, a fielder's easy throw to a nearby base.

First-baseman Rodrigo Hernandez gives a soft toss to Pitcher, Alonzo Humberto for the out.

Solo Home Run

Meaning: A home run with no one on base.

The slugger from Louisiana slams a solo home run to put his team on the scoreboard in the bottom of the fifth inning.

Southpaw

Meaning: A Pitcher who pitches with his left hand/arm.

Looks like Manager Ted Parker is bringing Southpaw, Hideki Sumatra, to face the lefty, Julio Gomez.

Souvenir

Meaning: A batted ball foul into the spectator area.

It's a long fly ball to left, curving foul...souvenir.

Speed Merchant

Meaning: A Player who is exceptionally fast, especially on the base paths.

Speed merchant, Ronnie Kim, will be the Alley Cats' pinch runner for Third-baseman Clancy McDougal.

Spike Curveball

Meaning: A curve thrown with the index finger pulled out of the way and the knuckle up, pushing the ball.

Peppertree was frozen at the plate when a spike curveball was thrown for a strike.

Spikes/Cleats

Meaning: Steel or synthetic blade-protrusions extending downward from the soles of baseball shoes, to provide a Player grip on composite-dirt and grass.

Martinelli slid into second, cleats up, attempting to break up the double play, and both he and the Batter, Axton, were called out for the rules infraction; Martinelli also being ejected from the game.

Spitball/Spitter

Meaning: In this now-illegal pitch, the Pitcher smears saliva or some other foreign substance on the ball, purposefully causing it to have erratic movement.

Umpires across the league are on the hunt to catch Pitcher Walter Landis throwing his notorious spitter.

Split-finger/Splitter

Meaning: Thrown with the Pitcher's fingers spread widely on the ball; this pitch looks like a fastball but drops radically before reaching the strike zone. *Distinguish,* Sinker

Taylor has a nasty splitter and the bottom really dropped outta that pitch to Carlson.

Spoil (a pitch)/Stay Alive

Meaning: With two strikes on the count, to foul off a terribly difficult pitch in order to avoid a strikeout at the plate.

Beamon spoiled that four-seamer on the outside corner to stay alive in the bottom of the eighth inning.

Spray Hitter

Meaning: A Batter with the capability of hitting to multiple areas of the field for base hits. *See,* Slap Hitter

The scrappy Shortstop, Bernard Alcaraz, is a very dangerous spray hitter, and the Sand Dollar infield is playing him straight away.

Squared Up

Meaning: When a Batter positions both feet facing the Pitcher, in preparation for a bunt attempt.

Marsden squares up, bunts the ball down the third baseline and…beats out the throw to first.

Squeeze Play/Safety Squeeze

Meaning: A bunt play, before there are two outs, where the primary goal is to advance a runner from third base to home plate (with a secondary goal for the Batter to reach first base safely) and the baserunner breaks for home after the bunt has been laid down. *Distinguish,* Sacrifice Bunt and Suicide Squeeze

There's the pitch, Purdy lays down a bunt and Timmons breaks for home…and the squeeze play ties up this ballgame!

Stance

Meaning: The manner in which a particular Batter sets up in the Batter's box, in preparation for each pitch.

Gage has an open stance in the box, but steps forward on the pitch, giving him a clear view of the ball and also the ability to cover that outside corner of the plate.

Stand-up (double or triple)

Meaning: A ball hit in such a manner as to allow the Batter to reach second or third base without the need to slide into that base.

And that rip to the right-center field gap is gonna be Pierce's second stand-up double for the game.

Starter/Starting Pitcher

Meaning: A team's Pitcher who pitches to the opposing team's first Batter of the first inning.

Tonight's Starting Pitchers will be Victor Eagleton for the Hawks and Spencer Quinella for the Lounge Lizards.

Station to Station

Meaning: The strategy, or outcome, of advancing runners one base at a time through any means available (*e.g.*, steal, bunting, fielder's choice, base hit and walk).

Yoder laid down the perfect bunt for the two baserunners to move station to station into scoring position.

Steal (a base) (verb)

Meaning: For a baserunner to advance to the next base safely when a pitch is made and the ball is not hit by the Batter, except when the advance is allowed by defensive indifference.

Youngblood snaps a throw to second and the steal is unsuccessful as Martinez dives but is tagged out at the bag.

Stealing Home

Meaning: As the term suggests, when the "base" to which a baserunner is attempting to advance, not by a batted ball, is home plate.

Hauser is always a threat to steal home—he's fast, can time the Pitcher's actions and has an uncanny ability to slide around tags.

Stealing Signs/Sign Stealing (*see also*, Peeking)

Meaning: Anyone affiliated with one team, seeing, hearing or otherwise figuring out the signals of another team, with the objective of timely passing the information on to his or her own affiliated team.

The Motor City Gear-heads' Bat-boy was apparently stealing signs from the Orca's Third Base Coach and passing those signs off to the Gear-heads' Batters in real time.

Stepping in the Bucket

Meaning: A bad habit, leading to a significant loss of power and accuracy in a Batter's swing, of the Batter's lead foot landing sideways, away from the plate during the swing.

Bartolli has developed a terrible habit of stepping in the bucket and if he doesn't correct that soon, his average will sink below the Mendoza Line.

Sticky Stuff

Meaning: Substances a Pitcher might use (against the rules of baseball) on the baseball to affect its flight—such as pine tar, saliva, resin and petroleum jelly.

That pitch had so much erratic movement, we may have some sticky stuff in play here, and that is exactly what the Umpire is looking for in an examination both of the ball and Pitcher Rich Pezman.

Stolen Base (noun)

Meaning: Where a baserunner has progressed to the next base in sequence, not as a result of a hit ball, error or defensive indifference.

The Rhinos already have three stolen bases today and with Pedro Martinez on first and two outs, they could be looking at a fourth any moment.

Stopper

Meaning: A team's best Starting Pitcher for shutting down a losing streak.

It's been a downward slide for the Penguins, on a nine-game losing streak, but they're bringing in Brad Horn as their stopper tonight.

Stop Sign

Meaning: When a Base Coach throws up both arms vertically, to signal a baserunner to not proceed further than the bag he just passed or is closely approaching.

Castanza ignored the stop sign, running all-out towards home and beat the tag by a micro-second.

Stranded/Left on Base/LOB

Meaning: Where one or more baserunners remain on base when a half-inning ends with the third out.

Once again, the visiting Jackrabbits failed to cash in on their hits, and left two stranded going into the bottom of the sixth inning.

The Stretch

Meaning: A compact pitching regimen designed to enable the Pitcher to more clearly see a baserunner's lead and to make a pick-off move if needed.

McCalley into the stretch, looks the runner back and the pitch—cutter for a called strike one.

Strike

Meaning: When the Batter swings and misses or tries to check his swing but it is called as having sufficiently crossed the plate, or swings and hits a foul ball (except on a third strike unless the ball is foul-tipped and caught by the Catcher, in which case it is a strike), or when the Batter doesn't swing but the pitch is called a "strike" by the Plate Umpire. For the Umpire to correctly call a pitch a strike, it must cross the plate within the strike zone as defined by the league rules.

Peterman stood frozen at the plate, bat held high above his head, waiting for the inevitable "strike" call by the Umpire.

Strike Him Out, Throw Him Out

Meaning: Any play where the Batter strikes out and the Catcher throws to a base, throwing out an advancing baserunner.

Aoki was fast, very fast, but it was strike him out, throw him out on a called third strike to his countryman, Masaru Asaji.

Strikeout/Rung Up (noun)

Meaning: Attributed to a *Batter*, when the Batter has three strikes without hitting the ball into fair territory.

Tinley had a miserable night at the plate, with a fly out and four strikeouts, two of which were looking.

Strikeout/ Punchout/Backwards K (for a third called strike)/K (for a third strike swinging) (noun)

Meaning: Attributed to a *Pitcher*, when a Batter has three strikes without hitting the ball into fair territory.

That's Ray Soldier's fourth punchout and we're still in the bottom of the third inning.

Strike Out/Fan/Punch Out (verb—*p.o.v.* Pitcher)

Meaning: The act of striking out a Batter. *See,* Rang Him Up

Rodriguez punches out Toyo for a one, two, three inning.

Strike Out Looking (verb)

Meaning: For a Batter to strike out when the third strike is a called-strike—*i.e.,* without the Batter offering at the ball.

Fastball right through the heart of the plate and Thorpe strikes out looking for the first out of the inning.

Strike Out the Side

Meaning: In any given half-inning, to retire the side by strikeouts alone.

Rabinski allowed two hits this inning, but he also struck out the side and no runs scored.

Strikes Out/Striking Out (verb—*p.o.v.* Batter)

Meaning: The act of a Batter striking out in an at-bat.

At this point, McAnarney will be satisfied if he simply avoids striking out.

Strike Zone/Zone

Meaning: The imaginary, rectangular box immediately over home plate, starting at a Batter's knees and extending upward to just below the midpoint between a Batter's shoulders and the top of their pants when the Batter is in his natural batting stance, inside of which imaginary box if a pitched ball passes through any part of it, the pitch should be considered as a strike even if the Batter doesn't swing his bat.

This Umpire wouldn't know the strike zone if someone hit him over the head with it, and that's putting it mildly.

Stuff

Meaning: A Pitcher's ability to throw deceptive and diverse pitches.

For certain, Madison had his stuff in his last start, but today, his stuff is nowhere to be found.

Suicide Squeeze

Meaning: With less than two outs, the runner on third base breaks for home plate, and the Batter squares to bunt the ball, just prior to the Pitcher's release to home plate. Distinguish, Sacrifice Bunt and Squeeze Play

With the count two and one, and Purdy with a strong lead from third, Simmons releases a 4-seamer and the suicide squeeze is on!

Suspended Game

Meaning: When a game is tied and has progressed far enough to constitute a regulation game, but must be called, due to any number of causes, and resumed at a later date.

At the top of the eighth inning, a score of 6-6 and the onslaught of a relentless blizzard, the game between the Rochester Rockers and the St Paul Saints was unceremoniously suspended.

Sweep

Meaning: For a team to win every game of a series of games against an opposing team.

The Carmel Turtles annihilated the Fort Wayne Felines in a four-game sweep.

Sweeper

Meaning: A pitch with a large amount of horizontal movement, and less break than a slider.

The rookie, Archibald Crutchfield, introduced the sweeper pitch that worked in the Minors and was taking the Majors by storm.

Sweet Spot (of the bat)

Meaning: The meat of the bat, near the end, although not the very end of the business end of the bat; the area where Batters want to contact the pitched ball.

With the sweet spot of the bat, Terrence hammered that ball to the left field foul pole, and he'll have himself a stand-up triple.

Swing/Offer (verb)

Meaning: For a Player to attempt to hit a baseball pitched to him by a Pitcher in the course of a baseball game.

Peterson offered at the pitch but it was a swing and a miss for strike three, and after four innings of play, the Eight Balls lead the Sky Fliers by a score of three to two.

Switch/Switch Hitter

Meaning: A Player who can bat right- or left-handed, depending on which arm, right or left, the Pitcher uses to pitch—so that if the Pitcher is left-handed, the Batter would bat right-handed, and *vice versa.*

Switch hitter Hank Gaffrey will bat right against the Danes' Southpaw hurler, Rowdy Cantor.

T

Tag Out/Tag

Meaning: When a baserunner is in jeopardy and not in contact with a base, for an opposing Player to tag him (out) with the ball directly or with a hand or glove holding the ball.

With the crowd-favorite hidden ball trick, Third-baseman Peewee James tagged out a surprised Bulldogs Player.

Tag Up/Tagging Up

Meaning: When a fly ball is caught, then at *or after* the moment of the catch, and before attempting to advance, each baserunner must contact the base they were at prior to the ball being batted; and after that catch, if any defensive Player in control of the ball touches that base before the baserunner touches it, the baserunner is out.

McNearney left the base early, before the catch, and on appeal, is called out for failure to tag up.

Tailor-made Double Play

Meaning: With a runner on first base, a well-hit grounder directly to either the Second-baseman or Shortstop, an easy feed to second and quick throw to first to beat the runner.

A one-bouncer to Short, the feed and a solid throw to first for a tailor-made double play to end the inning.

Take One for the Team/Wear (a pitch)

Meaning: Being hit by a pitch when efforts to avoid the ball are marginal, if that.

Vestermark turns away slightly and takes one for the team to the meat of his left arm, from an inside fastball.

Take the Field

Meaning: Each time the team playing defense proceeds from their dugout to their respective positions on the field.

When the Ramblers take the field in the bottom of the fourth inning, their new Pitcher will be Long-Reliever Jimmy, "Pops," Marin.

Talk Smack

Meaning: Overtly derogatory comments made by a Player or Players of one team, against a Player or Players of the opposing team.

Following a verbal warning, Catcher, Steve Sondheim, continued to talk smack to the Batter, Craig Carpinteria, and was promptly ejected from the game.

Tap

Meaning: For a Batter to inadvertently hit a ball lightly and without power

Ogilby taps the ball to third and is thrown out for the second out of the inning.

Tape-measure Home Run

Meaning: A ball that is batted very deeply into or over the outfield stands in fair territory.

Edgerton got every bit of that ball and it is outta here for a tape-measure home run!

Tattoo

Meaning: To bat a ball exceedingly hard so as to virtually mark the ball from the contact.

Bailey tattoos that ball into left-center field, it's off the wall, bounces past Right-fielder Patterson, and Bailey is into third with a stand-up triple.

Tea Party

Meaning: A mound visit where most or all of the infielders join into the conference, followed, inevitably, by the Home Plate Umpire.

In the tea party, the guys chatted about a shark movie they all wanted to see at a late-night cinema.

Third Base/Third

Meaning: The bag 90 feet to the left of home plate, third in a sequence of four, counting home plate.

Albert Tunney is rounding third like his feet are on fire and literally screams toward the plate, dives under the tag and is safe for the game-winning, walk-off run!

Third-baseman

Meaning: The Player assigned, on defense, to the infield position in the third base area.

They call him the vacuum cleaner—he's Bob Mariah, Third-baseman for the Cincinnati Flyers!

Three-bagger/Triple

Meaning: A hit where the Batter reaches third base safely, without any defensive error.

The fans know, we know and Buddy McKinzie certainly knows that what he needs now, what he wants now, is to hit a three-bagger to hit for the cycle.

Threw the Anchor Down

Meaning: When a baserunner, given the "stop" sign by a coach, or realizing that he will be tagged out if he continues toward the next base, stops rapidly and returns to the base he just passed.

Peterson rounded second on a full run but threw the anchor down when Third Base Coach, Andy Walker, frantically gave him the "stop" sign.

Throw a Dime

Meaning: A long throw from a fielder to a perfect spot for a tagout.

Winslow was out at the plate by a country mile when Bettleman threw a dime to Catcher Martin Alcala.

Throwing BBs/Throwing Gas/Throwing Heat/
Throwing Smoke/Throwing Cheeze

Meaning: For a Pitcher with a strong arm and good pitching mechanics to pitch high-velocity fastballs.

Satoshi is throwing BBs tonight and has fanned six Batters through four innings.

Thrown Out

Meaning: When a fielder, on a force play at a base, throws the ball and another Player catches the thrown ball and touches the base prior to the baserunner touching.

Mean Bill Green was charging toward first like a steam locomotive, but was thrown out by the agile Second-baseman, Krispy Klean.

Throws Left/Throws Right

Meaning: Referring to the arm of the defensive Player with which he throws the ball.

Zander Hitchkok throws left and the Dogtown Batters will have their hands full facing this pitching machine.

Tie Him Up/Tied Up

Meaning: When a pitch is so close to a Batter's hands, that it makes it very difficult for him to swing the bat.

Paxton tied him up with that inside cutter, and sawed off Coutier's bat.

Tomahawk (the ball)

Meaning: To hit a ball high in or over the strike zone by slicing down at it with the bat.

> *Bailey wanted him to climb the ladder for a strike, but Pearce turned the tables by tomahawking the ball into left-center field for a single.*

Tools of Ignorance

Meaning: Catcher's gear.

> *Jenkins takes Mitchell's warm-up pitches while Rankin dons his tools of ignorance.*

Top of the Order

Meaning: The first three Batters on the line-up card—the top of the order recurs during the game unless substitutions are made.

> *The Beagles are down three, at the bottom of the seventh, but the top of the order is coming up, so let's see what they can do.*

Torpedo Bat

Meaning: A wooden bat where the sweet-spot of the bat's barrel is enhanced in girth and the end of the barrel is shaved and sanded down somewhat.

> *The jury is out whether the pros outweigh the cons of a torpedo bat, but most Players will give a try.*

Tossed

Meaning: A Player, Coach or Manager having been ejected from a game by an Umpire for perceived misbehavior.

> *The Batter drawing a line in the dirt was all it took, and the Blue tossed him without hesitation.*

Touch All the Bases/Touch 'Em All

Meaning: For a Player to hit a Home Run.

> *And for the 32nd time this season, powerhouse Designated Hitter, Hajime Osaka, gets to touch 'em all!*

Track Down

Meaning: For an outfielder to physically follow the trajectory of a fly ball in order to make the catch.

> *That ball is a rocket off Moroski's bat, but Severson tracks it down and makes the catch to close out the inning.*

Trap the Ball

Meaning: Not an actual catch on the fly, but where the ball, or some portion thereof, is pinned to the ground by the fielder's glove.

> *An amazing effort, but the call on the field is that Moravek trapped the ball.*

Triple Play

Meaning: A very uncommon play, with no outs and at least two baserunners on base, where the fielders accomplish three outs in a single at-bat.

Line drive caught; Third-baseman, Ed Cruise, throw to Crosby at second, and on to Nicholson at first, for a triple play.

Turn a Double Play/Turn Two/Tinker to Evers to Chance (verb)

Meaning: A particular double play where an infielder fields a batted ball, throws the ball to a base for a force or tag out, and the fielder who catches that throw, throws the ball to another base (typically first base) for an additional force or tag out.

Ground ball to Short and it's "Tinker to Evers to Chance" for outs two and three of the 8th inning.

Two-bagger/Double

Meaning: Where the Batter hits a pitched ball and arrives at second base safely, with no errors attributable to the defense.

That line drive is tipped by the First-baseman's glove, Purvis is waved around first and has himself a two-bagger.

Two-seam Fastball/Two-seamer

Meaning: A slightly slower fastball than a four-seam fastball, seen by a Batter to have two seams, rather than four, and breaking slightly down and toward the Pitcher's throwing side.

That's a two-seamer, ripped into the left-center gap for a stand-up double.

Tying run

Meaning: The baserunner or run which moves or would move the team on offense into tie.

Ground ball through the infield and the Knights are aboard with the tying run at first.

u

Ugly Finder

Meaning: A foul ball, hit into a dugout, scattering the occupants.

An ugly finder ripped into the visitor's dugout and it was every man for himself in there!

Umpire/Ump/Blue

Meaning: An official on the playing field.

Umpire Tom Spleckinheimer was infamous for his grossly-inflated strike zone.

Unassisted Play

Meaning: When a defensive Player completes an out by himself.

Taylor gloves a short-hop at third, steps on the bag for an unassisted play and we go to the bottom of the fifth inning.

Uncle Charlie

Meaning: Nickname for a curveball pitch, as a dig to Charles W. Elliot, the Harvard President who felt that a deceptive pitch should neither be permitted nor encouraged in baseball.

Georgios goes down swinging on an Uncle Charlie and now it's time for the seventh inning stretch.

Uncontested Steal/Defensive Indifference

Meaning: Where a baserunner is attempting to steal the next base, but because of other circumstances, a Catcher chooses not to attempt to throw him out.

Kim takes off for second on Brody's move to the plate, but that will be scored as defensive indifference with the rabbit, Buster Millicent, on third.

Unearned Run/Unearned

Meaning: A run scored which, in the judgement of the official scorer, is attributed to a fielding error or a passed ball, and not counted in the Pitcher's statistics of runs scored against him.

Robles touches all four, but one of the three RBIs will be unearned, thanks to the earlier fielding error by Second-baseman, Jocko Smith.

Uno, Dos, Adios

Meaning: Translated into English from Spanish—one (out), two (outs), goodbye—a Spanish language equivalent of "three up, three down."

Uno, dos, adios Coyotes.

Up and In

Meaning: Any pitch that is both high and inside, often intended by the Pitcher to back the Batter off of the plate and to set up the next low and away pitch.

Kentama serves up chin music to Walters, up and in, and Walters is not having it—there he goes, he's charging the mound!

Upper Decker

Meaning: A home run hit so far that it lands in an "upper deck" of the baseball stadium.

Oh, that was a blast by Ramos—an upper decker, one of the highest and longest of this season.

Upstairs/High

Meaning: Any pitch crossing above the strike zone.

It was a hair high, and called a ball by Home Plate Umpire Sergio Diaz.

Up the Middle

Meaning: The direction of a batted ball, generally over and past second base.

Yammer blasts one up the middle, driving in a run and arriving safely at first base.

Utility Player

Meaning: A Player who, on defense, can effectively play multiple fielding positions, according to the needs of the team.

Utility Player Sergio Alcatraz is playing center field today and is batting five for twelve in the past three games.

Vacuum

Meaning: An infielder who has particularly good fielding skills.

Rambo was a vacuum and could get to nearly anything in the third base zone.

Visit/Visitor/Visiting

Meaning: When a team plays another team on the other team's home field and bats in the top half of the innings.

Visiting team tonight is the Phoenix Bull Dogs and their record is one of the tops at this level of the Minors.

Wait On It

Meaning: Solid advice given hitters by batting coaches, to delay starting the swing as long as possible in order to have that little extra time to see what the pitch is doing and then to make a decisive swing with fast hands to deliver power to the batted ball.

One thing I learned in adult, amateur baseball, is to wait on it when batting and then hit it hard to any field the pitch allows.

Walk-off

Meaning: Any hit in the bottom of the 9th- or later-inning which wins the game for the home team.

Mitchell has a 1 and 2 count, probably sitting on a fastball, the pitch and—rip to right-center for a walk-off single!

Warning Track

Meaning: A wide area of dirt and synthetic material bordering the playing field's back wall and sidelines, designed to alert a fielder that a solid obstruction is close.

Sampson goes back, he's at the warning track, leaps up and robs Lucchesi of a home run.

Waste a Pitch

Meaning: When the Pitcher is ahead in the count, he may deliberately throw a pitch outside of the strike zone to attempt to have the Batter chase it.

Hunter threw that one way outside the strike zone and he wanted to waste a pitch, see if Pederson would chase—but it didn't happen.

Wave (a runner)/Wave On/Go Sign/Waved Around

Meaning: When a Base Coach signals, by circling-around one arm vertically (high-to-low-to high etc.), a baserunner to continue running toward the next base.

It's off the wall and Warner has waved Purdy who will be... out at third in a very close play.

Went Fishing

Meaning: When a Batter's swing reached across the plate attempting to hit an outside pitch, but missed the ball.

Oliver went fishing on that cutter and the count goes to O and 2.

Wheelhouse

Meaning: That area of the strike zone which, for the particular Batter, is just right for a powerful swing on the pitched ball.

That hanging curve was right in Turner's wheelhouse, and it is way gone!

Wheels

Meaning: A fast Player's legs.

Stripling has the wheels, rounds third for home, and the throw is—not in time!

Whiff

Meaning: Swinging at but missing the pitched ball completely.

Big-time whiff for Matoff, and the count's 2 and 2.

Wild Pitch

Meaning: Essentially, the equivalent of a Pitcher's error in the pitch itself, which gets by the Catcher and could not be caught with ordinary effort.

That's the second wild pitch for Ezekiel, and this time, it cost the Antelopes a run.

Window Shopping

Meaning: A Batter taking a third strike with no apparent effort to swing.

Elgin Carson caught window shopping for the third out of the inning.

Windup/Wind

Meaning: A pitching regimen incorporating a momentary "set" position, followed by swinging motion of the arms and a front leg "kick," all designed to enable the most powerful pitches.

Price in his windup and it's a slider to the lower outside corner—strike one.

Work the Count

Meaning: For a Batter to be careful about chasing and to foul off multiple pitches which were on the margins of the strike zone, improving the chances of getting a good pitch to hit, and also, adding to the Pitcher's pitch count.

Huntley is a master at working the count and in this at-bat alone Verdugo has thrown 13 pitches, with the count still full.

Worm Burner

Meaning: A ground ball hit so hard and low that it seems it could burn the grass along the way.

That was a worm burner and its no wonder why Aruba was unable to pick it clean.

y

Yips

Meaning: A Player's mysterious loss of control of his throws.

O'Leary has a serious case of the yips tonight, with three walks, a hit-by-pitch and a wild pitch through one and a third innings.

You Hang 'Em, We Bang 'Em

Meaning: If your Pitcher throws a breaking ball pitch which gently curves right into the heart of the zone, then our Batters will jump all over those pitches for extra-base hits and home runs.

And Tinsley goes yiketty yak on a hanging curve—"You hang 'em, we bang 'em!"

z

Zinger

Meaning: A very hard-hit line-drive base hit.

Hideki Masunama was in an O for 14-slump but he just hit a zinger to break that drought.